Absolute Leadership

THE SIX COMPETENCIES

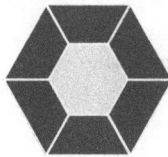

Joseph Tigani

National Library of Australia Cataloguing-in-Publication entry
    Author: Tigani, Joseph
    Title: Absolute leadership: the six competencies / Joseph Tigani.
    ISBN: 9780980637113 (pbk.)
    Subjects: Leadership. Core competencies.
    Dewey Number: 658.4

Absolute Leadership
is based upon respect and dignity
for oneself and for others.

Preface

Absolute Leadership consists of six competencies essential to transforming your possibilities into reality. By developing the six competencies, you can take much greater charge of your own destiny, lift your career and business to far more satisfying levels, and accomplish the aspirations and goals that are important to you, to your teams, business and organization. You can expect similar benefits in your private life.

The starting point is to be able to lead yourself. Once you gain clarity about what really matters to you and the direction you would like to take, then that serves as the basis to develop the necessary skills to inspire other people to willingly follow you as a leader.

Always conduct yourself with trust and respect for other people. This is critical in a world with less reliance upon power based hierarchies and increasing emphasis on effectively engaging with people in teams and net-works, across and between organizations and countries.

Since Absolute Leadership emphasizes what people actually do and can become, it is suitable for almost anyone in any sized organization, from a one-person business to a global corporation. It equally applies to teams, networks and organizations.

As a leadership coach and trainer, I have observed firsthand how the six competencies produce rewarding outcomes for anyone, any team and any organization, that applies them. The opportunity to do likewise is up to you.

Joseph Tigani

Contents

Introduction

"If you do not know where you are going, any road will get you there."

Lewis Carroll, English writer, 1832 - 1898

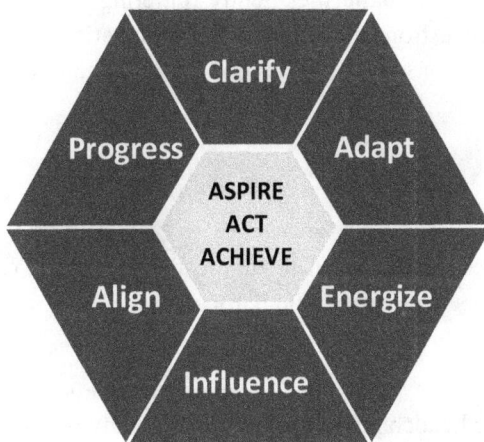

The award

Just pause for a moment. Imagine it is ten years from now.

You are at a formal presentation night where you are about to be presented with a leadership award in recognition of your exceptional achievements as a leader over the preceding ten years. The atmosphere is buzzing with the energy of leaders from many different industries and organizations, including your own. As well, your spouse or partner is sitting at the front table in your full view from where you stand on stage alongside the Master of Ceremonies who is about to introduce you to the audience.

As is customary with these awards, you have been asked to make a speech about your role as a leader in the ten years leading up to your award. Your speech is to outline your leadership achievements over those years, including the initiatives you have undertaken; what you have learnt; the impacts you have made on the lives of others; the value you have brought to your organization and your industry; the people who have played a vital role in your achievements; and the high points.

The Master of Ceremonies introduces you to the audience and motions for you to move to the podium. As you stand there, you feel the heat of the spotlight upon your face. A few drops of perspiration form on your forehead. You can feel butterflies gently fluttering in your stomach. There is a hush of silence from the audience in anticipation of your words. The moment to make your speech has arrived. What do you say?

Definition

To make the acceptance speech for the leadership award requires that you have been a competent leader. The purpose of this book is to enable you to develop your Absolute Leadership, defined as follows:

> "Absolute Leadership guides and unites individuals to willingly
> act to achieve collectively shared and valued outcomes".

For you to guide and unite individuals to follow a direction, you must be clear regarding the direction to take. It starts with clarity about your own direction. If you do not know your own direction, do not expect others to follow you. If you would not follow others, who do not know where they are leading you, it is unrealistic to expect anyone to do the same with you. Leading others requires that you can lead yourself first. Others may then follow if they are confident of the direction you propose, the actions you take, and the trust you have engendered. It does not matter that initially you may not know the exact path, as what is essential to begin with is for you to have a clear sense of destination or direction.

Absolute Leadership is not just about you as an individual. It is also about your teams, the organization for which you work, plus people outside of work, especially your family, community and society. All of those people are connected either directly or indirectly to each other, with you as the common link between them. As a leader your role is a pivotal one. Accordingly, your personal conduct as leader must have regard to the collective values of those other people in whatever situations occur.

'Willingly' means that people do things voluntarily. In the case of Absolute Leadership, people follow because they want to, as opposed to being forced or in some way coerced to come along and take part. However, some individuals may find it difficult to comprehend the direction taken by a leader or organization, whilst others may well understand but not be at all interested in pursuing that path. For them, other choices and opportunities are ultimately available, as leadership does not mean that everyone that can will necessarily want to be involved.

The word 'achieve' indicates that there must be a means of ascertaining what progress is made and when outcomes are actually fulfilled. 'Collectively shared and valued' emphasizes that Absolute Leadership benefits everyone involved by providing something of value to the participants. How the interests of all stakeholders will be affected needs to be taken into account, notwithstanding that resolutions have to be found for managing what are often competing interests between different groups, as for example between the interests of employees and shareholders. If one stakeholder group suffers at the expense of another group, it reflects a lack of collectively shared respect for the afflicted group. The lack of respect undermines leadership. The 'outcomes' to work towards must be articulated, made known to those being led or proposed to be led, and be pursued.

Core principles

Three notions integral to and part of the Absolute Leadership competencies are to Aspire, to Act, and to Achieve. These form the three core principles of Absolute Leadership.

Aspire

To aspire is to seek a career and life that has personal meaning, purpose and value.

Act

To act is to take actions and conduct yourself in a manner consistent with your aspirations. If your actions do not initially achieve your intended outcomes then you can adjust or change what you do.

Achieve

To achieve is to accomplish or fulfill your intended purpose and the outcomes you seek in accordance with your aspirations. It is to become and experience what you aspire to be.

The three principles actively link to each other. Actions must be aligned with aspirations and be monitored as to how well they progress you towards your aspirations. That is partly why you will find an emphasis on personal conduct, and the rewarding of actions rather than just outcomes, as a vital element of Absolute Leadership.

If your actions do not achieve your aspirations, you need to reconsider your actions and change what you are doing. There is no point to keep on doing what does not work, yet many people fall into the trap of doing exactly what they have always done but foolishly expecting a different result. Many people also fall into the easy option of giving up on their aspirations when their initial actions do not succeed. In turn they never get to experience the achievement of meaning, purpose and value, instead succumbing to something far less than they are truly capable.

The ultimate responsibility for your own career, life, and business, rests with you. It is up to you to make the effort to identify the purpose of your life and to select the direction and path you take. If you do not choose your own direction, then someone else, or 'circumstances', will choose it for you. You need to be able to confidently say, "I am taking this direction (whatever you decide to do), for this reason (why you have decided upon your chosen direction)." In addition, you also need to know when you achieve your aspirations in the context of your own work and private life.

Once you clarify what has personal meaning and purpose you can then begin taking actions to fulfill your aspirations. You can also implement measures to assess whether your actions progress you towards your aspirations. This will help you from a career or business perspective, to work more effectively with others to achieve the aspirations of the various teams you are involved with, as well as the aspirations and goals of your business or organization. So in brief, you can apply Absolute Leadership individually, with your teams, and with the people across your networks, business and organization.

Meaningful aspirations

The first core principle of Absolute Leadership is to identify what you intend to do, and why, in order to give meaning to your aspirations.

Whatever you aspire to professionally and in your private life should define what you would truly like to become, based upon the personal values that shape your aspirations. Aspirations extend beyond business and career to all other domains or aspects of your life, such as your partner relationship and family, social and community activities, spirituality and religion, finances, health and fitness.

A critical part of aspirations is your awareness of the possibilities available to you. The possibilities are limited only by your imagination and willingness to pursue them. It takes courage! If you need proof of that, just look at some of the great leaders who have risen from poverty and obscurity to take the leaders' stage in their chosen area.

Whatever you can imagine is actually possible, otherwise you would not be able to imagine it. That in itself is good reason to use all of your powers of imagination to envisage aspirations that genuinely resonate with you, that are what you really want to do, that are truly what you want to be, that reflect the success you want to achieve, and that because they are so important you are prepared to put in the necessary effort to transform your aspirations into reality.

Intentional actions

The second core principle of Absolute Leadership is to act. It means taking appropriate actions and behaviors necessary to achieve your aspirations. To make your actions relevant and effective, direct them towards fulfilling your aspirations so you can lead the career and life that you imagine. It is by taking actions that you become the person, and the leader, who you aspire to be. Action starts with identifying the steps that you will take and aligning those action steps with your long-term aspirations (at least five years or more from now) and short-term goals (within two years from now, but preferably within the next twelve months). Align your actions with your strategy as an individual, but also ensure to align your actions with the aspirations of your teams and organization.

Since aspirations have a strong, positive, emotive element, personally meaningful aspirations are a powerful internal driving force behind actions. There is a dynamic and forceful link between meaningful aspirations and purposeful actions. A lack of clear and meaningful aspirations causes a lack of purposeful actions. To know what to do, and to do anything well, is a lot easier if you know the reason or motivation behind it.

All too often people are 'busy being busy' at work, but they do not actually accomplish very much of value, or they do not accomplish as much or add as much value as they are capable. Often that is due to their actions not being aligned with their intended outcomes or results. In many cases, they are so busy that they actually lose sight of the intended results or targets to which they profess to be working. Hence, they lose sight of the very purpose behind their actions. A consequence is that 'busy being busy' type activities become their purpose, rather than using activities to achieve higher value outcomes.

Absolute Leaders recognize that the economic value of time is determined by productivity. They minimize time wasting by allocating their time effectively and by making the most valuable use of their time. One way they attain that is to establish priorities using a plan, so that they are both effective and efficient. Most importantly, in order to be clear about what they are working to achieve, they apply business planning methods to help them put into perspective the purpose and value of their actions.

Rewarding achievements

Achievement is the third core principle of Absolute Leadership. When you achieve something, you become what you achieve. Hence, achieving an aspiration is experiencing it. Achieving is a feeling and an emotion that gives you a sense of satisfaction.

Achievements must produce a sense of reward. They should make you feel good about yourself because of what you have done, the way you have conducted yourself, and the benefits they produce for others as well as yourself. If you achieve something and it does not give you a sense of pride and accomplishment, then ask yourself why. Perhaps what you were doing and the outcome of it did not really matter to you.

Working deliberately towards accomplishing your aspirations will allow you to reflect, at any future time, whether you are leading a life and experiencing a career (or several different careers over the course of your working life) that gives you personal meaning, value, and genuine satisfaction. In short, it is the satisfaction of achieving what you really want to do with your life, rather than living the life someone else dictates to you.

The six competencies

The six competencies of Absolute Leadership are the ability to: (i) Clarify; (ii) Adapt; (iii) Energize; (iv) Influence; (v) Align, and; (vi) Progress.

To be competent in something means to be able to do it especially well. A competent Absolute Leader, therefore, is able to consistently perform the six competencies at a highly skilful level, and with all types of people, in an expansive range of situations.

Clarify

Clarity of your purpose and your aspirations is accomplished through connecting what you do with the personal values that drive or motivate you. It is being true to yourself. It is imagining a clear vision of what you aspire to, expanding your range of paradigms so you can perceive the world and situations differently, and being aware of your perceptions. It all helps create the motivation within you to act in accordance with your purpose, being whatever helps you attain and experience genuine satisfaction with your work and personal life. Vision on its own is not enough to create your ideal rewarding life in the physical world, unless it links to the critical values that guide your aspirations, actions and behavior.

Adapt

Change, and the ability to adapt to change, is required for progress if we are to move forward and away from where things are or were previously. The whole world is constantly changing at every moment, so the notion that we do not have to adapt ourselves to change not only defies logic but it defies the entire history of the world! How we handle change and adapt ourselves depends upon our expectations, our personal self-beliefs, and the paradigms through which we view change in order that we adapt, survive and prosper.

Expectations often become self-fulfilling prophecies. If you expect something better to happen in the future, it most likely will. Alternatively, if you expect something worse, then that will most likely happen. Expecting positive outcomes makes all the difference. Whether you realize it or not, whatever you expect is a choice you make. Being stuck in the past is of little or no help to your present or to your future because it cannot be relived. There is no point in having any regrets about the past because it cannot be changed.

Absolute Leaders move forward through positive action, self-belief and self-confidence, overcoming any myths that can limit their personal growth and development. Utilizing talents and strengths plus addressing weaknesses is vital. In making decisions, Absolute Leaders also make the critical progression from over reliance upon information to skillfully applying wisdom and using their intuition.

Many people fear change, but Absolute Leaders prosper through change by accepting and utilizing it for growth, new opportunities and security. They adapt themselves as circumstances change, or they adapt in anticipation of changes in the world and situations around them. By adapting and being flexible, Absolute Leaders not only survive, but they are far more likely to flourish, prosper and thrive, as will the people whom they support, and whom in turn support them.

Energize

Energy activates the motion necessary for achievement. There are many ways that you can energize yourself to accelerate your personal growth and progress. Amongst those are harnessing the power of positive emotions, forming beneficial new habits, being persistent yet flexible, learning to visualize, using practical creativity, celebrating accomplishments, plus letting go of self-limiting practices such as unnecessarily blaming others or yourself. You can also find unlimited energy through maintaining a healthy diet, regular exercise and using stress management techniques such as meditation.

Your personal energy radiates to other people and it affects them. People pick up or tune into the positive or negative vibes of others. They sense the power of the personal energy someone brings into an environment and they respond accordingly to the climate or atmosphere created by the collective energy of individuals.

Influence

At the heart of influencing others is the ability to connect with others. Across career, team and organizational perspectives, Absolute Leaders focus upon, understand and engage in effective interactions with other people. By doing so they differentiate between leading and managing other people, in that leading is doing the right things to progress in the right direction, whereas managing is doing things right. Absolute Leaders empower others and they use feedback constructively as part of their repertoire of leadership skills. They relate well to the different generations in the workplace, they act affirmatively to optimize performance, and they exert influence, as for example by advantageously navigating the dynamics of power and politics in the workplace.

Communication is essential to effectively deal with other people. Conflicts can exist anywhere, and, contrary to what many people believe, conflicts need not be destructive. They are often very constructive especially if well managed. There are a number of conflict negotiation styles based upon the value or importance attributed to outcomes and relationships. Successful negotiating is enhanced by relating to people using effective communication skills, encompassing verbal and non-verbal communication, a critical element being the ability to actively listen.

Align

Absolute Leadership recognizes the vital role of aligning individuals, teams, networks and organizations at the aspirational, action and achievement levels. Teams are used increasingly throughout, across and between organizations, and in some cases replace traditional hierarchies. Internal and external networks are a vital source of potential advantage for individuals, teams and organizations. The resulting synergies of individuals working collaboratively as teams and networks to achieve common or shared purposes can catapult everyone involved to higher levels of performance and achievement that are otherwise unattainable by individuals working independently.

Customers are at the heart of any business or organization, and both the realization of who they are and the view you take towards your customers has a major impact upon your engagement, communication and transactions with them. Similarly, it is essential to understand who your stakeholders actually are, as well as the extent of power and influence they can exert upon you.

Irrespective of whatever you do for a career, managing yourself as a business with clear aims and goals can be of enormous assistance. Managing your career and life more effectively as a business is considerably easier to do by applying business planning principles, since the business planning process requires carefully considering your career or business destination and the pathways to get you there. In turn, that helps you better appreciate the value and priorities of your time so that you can achieve what you set out to do.

Progress

By measuring and assessing your progress you can monitor that your actions are on track to achieve your intended outcomes. You must make sure that what you do is effective in that what you do actually brings about the results you desire. It is also important to consider progress in the context of those people you supervise and who are in your teams, as, for example, what opportunities you create for them to develop their own leadership and team participation abilities.

Constructive feedback from others with whom you work is critical for your leadership development. You will never really know your progress unless it is assessed and you make yourself accountable. You invest significant time, effort and money into your career, so make it personally rewarding and satisfying to know that you achieve your aspirations. Your organization also invests significantly in you so it is essential that you perform to the best of your potential to at least fulfill, but preferably exceed, the performance requirements of your professional role.

Collaboration, trust and respect

Absolute Leadership is a complete, holistic form of leadership, but it is not meant to be all things to all people.

In its application to teams, leadership includes not just the team leader but all members of the team, since all team members are required to participate in the proper functioning of the team if it is to achieve its goals.

In its application to businesses and organizations, leadership must embrace and encompass everyone within them, so that everyone feels there is a worthwhile direction with a leader and leadership group able to unite and guide everyone towards organizational missions and goals. It is up to individuals to lead within the context of their position within a team or organization and to opportunistically lead in the context of positions they aspire to be in despite not actually occupying those positions. Put another way, if you want to be a leader you must begin acting like one immediately. If you aspire to a higher position or advancement in your career or organization, then you can help yourself by beginning to consider matters from that higher level perspective.

Absolute Leadership is universal in its application, as well as global. It can be applied to any organization however large or small, from a one person enterprise to a global conglomerate. It applies not only to business enterprises, but also to government and non government organizations. It is applicable, regardless of industry and what type of product or service an organization provides.

The essential nature of Absolute Leadership is not coercion or force, but rather positive collaboration, trust, dignity and respect. In that way, Absolute Leadership really has no limitation to its effectiveness other than the ability of individuals to apply its six competencies and be committed to developing the competencies to their full potential. It is far more than just a leadership journey; it is about arriving at a leadership destination.

COMPETENCY 1
Clarify your purpose

"The secret of success is consistency of purpose."

Benjamin Disraeli, British statesman, 1804 - 1881

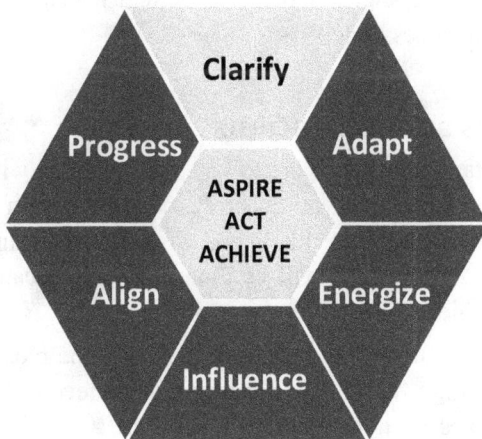

Values

Understanding your personal values is critical to your career and personal life, since values can either constrain or catapult your progress. Either way it all depends upon you. The starting point is to be aware of your values and appreciate how they substantially define what you believe, what you do, who you are, and who you become.

Values can be categorized as being either Aspirational, Action, or Achievement oriented values. Aspirational values are concerned with your ultimate purpose, which is whatever has most meaning for you. Action values relate to the behaviors you take or how you do things to progress yourself in the direction of your aspirations. Achievement values are what you feel or experience when your aspirations become reality.

Personal alignment

Alignment of personal actions with aspirations makes achievement not only possible, but also highly likely. The same also applies to aligning personal values with those of your workplace teams and your organization. In the process that leads to a better understanding and management of potential conflicts between values.

Align actions and aspirations

The more important your values are to you, the more you will be inclined to align your values with what you do professionally in your career or business, therefore the greater the likelihood of achieving your career aspirations and goals. Your actions will be more effective because they will be more suited to achieving whatever you aspire.

Actions that fully align with aspirations are the most powerful. Actions that do not align will simply not help you achieve your intended aspirations or outcomes. Actions that partly align are a step in the right direction, but complete alignment of actions with aspirations is what maximizes outcomes and is undoubtedly the best 'alignment solution'.

The more your actions and values align, the more that they are both 'in sync', then the more you will be able to resolve any conflicts between your values and what you actually do. Indeed, you will find that there is less and less conflict until eventually there is none.

For any one of your values, consider how you apply that value in your professional role. What are the benefits of the value to you? How do people around you benefit from your value? How do you actually apply that value? How is the value reflected through your interactions with others? What does that value mean to you as a leader? The value can be demonstrated by how you actually spend your time and what you accomplish. Through your actions and your priorities, the importance of any particular value becomes evident as do your other values and beliefs.

You, your teams and your organization

To facilitate your development of Absolute Leadership within the context of your business or organization, as far as possible align or reconcile your values with those of your organization, otherwise you could be working at cross purposes and that will only serve to block or limit your progress. In some cases, where such alignment is not at all possible or the 'value gap' between you and your organization is too wide to bridge, your position may be unsustainable and your best solution may be to join another organization.

Aligning with your organization involves comparing and assessing your values with those of your organization as far as similarities and differences are concerned. The next stage is to resolve any major conflicts or inconsistencies between your personal values and your organization's values that you believe will affect your performance. If major conflicts between your career values and your organization's values are not resolved they will constantly undermine your ability to perform in your role to your full potential and you will under achieve. So will the business. On the other hand, resolving the conflicts will form a solid base for your progress, fast tracking of your career, and deriving far greater enjoyment from your role.

For example, if one of your values is communication, look for ways in which there might be opportunities for you to practice and develop communication within your position. The opportunities could involve new communication initiatives such as a newsletter, blog, organizational intranet, or round table meeting.

Alignment of values also applies to leading or participating in teams. As with your organization, it is vital to align your values and resolve any major inconsistencies between your personal values and your teams' values, otherwise the functionality of you and your teams can be undermined. Once aligned, you are in a position to assist others to do the same, thereby contributing to the success of the team. In leading others, you can show them how they can connect their own values with those of their teams and their organization by relating how you have done so.

The more people who interact and work with each other appreciate the clarity of value connection and alignment between themselves, the more motivated they will usually be to work towards achieving team and organizational aims. It is also helpful to acknowledge the differences.

The pragmatic element to this is to understand that alignment of personal with team or organizational values seldom results in a 'perfect match'. In the absence of another alternative, often we may have to accept working with whom and with what we are presented even though we may have other preferences. It is a matter of being sufficiently tolerant and flexible, dealing with what is at hand, of dealing with what is actual rather than ideal. To paraphrase an analogy, you may just have to play with the cards that you are dealt.

Values, conscience and beliefs

Values can function as a personal protective mechanism. When required to do something in conflict with our values, we usually feel the resistance of something deep within us that questions that we think should be done. That resistance is an internal conflict that happens as a thought or inner voice before taking the action. When that occurs we become aware of an inconsistency within us that goes to our core beliefs, to the very essence of who we are, and it makes us feel uneasy. It is our conscience talking to us, questioning and challenging us, as to whether or not we are doing the right thing as far as what is right for us. At that juncture, we have the choice to either listen to our conscience and heed its message, or to go against it. The course we take depends upon how important it is in relation to our values to either do, or not do, what we are being asked. Ultimately that involves a trade-off between our values and the requested action and that is best considered in the context of the situation.

Since different people have different values, what is right for one person is not necessarily right for someone else. Therein lies a potential source of conflict with others, or more specifically a potential conflict between your values and those of other people. For example, you may be asked to do things that you do not feel comfortable with at work, but someone else may have no hesitation performing those same actions themselves, or asking someone else to do them. When something does not feel right to you but appears comfortable for someone else, it reflects a difference in personal values and beliefs between you and the other person. This highlights that even though we can belong to the same team or organization, each of us brings a different set of values to the workplace. The same applies in social situations. We each believe in different things and different ways of doing things. Although some of our values unite us because they are similar or can be reconciled, others can divide us if they are not reconciled. That in itself creates potential for conflicts and challenges, as we seek to fulfill our aspirations by being true to our innermost selves whilst at the same time striving to be effective leaders and team players cognizant of the aspirations of others with whom we interact and of the organizations where we work.

Values, beliefs and personal growth

We intuitively know when anything we do fits well with our values and beliefs because it feels right. In such instances we act automatically without questioning what we are doing. We are comfortable when there is an obvious action to take and it feels right to us.

Poorly evaluated or unconsidered personal values, however well in-tentioned they might be, can impede personal development. They can stop people doing things that might otherwise be helpful for their personal or professional growth. For example, people who believe that 'it is wrong to be wrong' might never admit to a mistake. They will often take the only escape routes seemingly available to them, being either total denial or to blame others for their own mistakes. As people naturally and quite rightly do not like to be blamed for someone else's shortcomings, those that do not admit to mistakes quickly alienate other people and often find themselves working in isolation (even though they may literally be surrounded by oth-ers) when they would benefit from the assistance of other people. Others will not voluntarily help or follow such people; they will only help if it is a requirement of their job or they are coerced to do so.

In the example of not admitting to a mistake, people holding the be-lief that 'it is wrong to be wrong' would benefit from re-evaluating its use-fulness, because, whether they admit it or not, it impedes their development and performance and affects that of other people with whom they interact. Rather than holding onto the belief that 'it is wrong to be wrong' it could be replaced with the leadership belief that 'it is OK to be wrong, just learn from the error and do not repeat it'. That type of value and belief shift is a mark of applied Absolute Leadership, highlighting that it is often wiser to be pragmatic rather than dogmatic with our values, especially when apply-ing our action values. That does not mean that we should continually com-promise our values, but it does necessitate that we understand in context the usefulness and practicality to us of the values that we hold and the beliefs that they underpin. In that way we can function pragmatically and effective-ly in the organizational and wider world in which we find ourselves.

Vision

Your aspirational vision is your mind's eye, or picture, of your future. It is your view of your future life and career. The clearer you make your vision in all aspects of your life, the sooner those aspects will materialize as you actually envision or imagine them to be. People who see their career and life vision clearer and earlier in life than others often achieve success earlier. Their vision becomes their life aim or objective and they begin working on transforming it into reality the moment they see or imagine it. This can be observed, for example, with sportspeople who start their chosen sport at a very young age, but it also happens with businesspeople, professional people, artists and trades people. In fact it can happen with anyone in any occupation or walk of life. How people envision themselves and their lives early on can have an enormous impact upon the career choices that they make and eventually upon their career and business success. If you do not have a clear vision then make it an absolute priority to become clear about what you want to achieve. Begin immediately to clarify your vision and by doing so it will help clarify your purpose.

One way to think of your vision is to imagine it as a movie picture that you carry within your mind at all times. Wherever you go, you take it with you. You are the director, the producer, the financier and the leading actor, all rolled into one person. No one else can create your movie for you, nor play your movie in their mind. You can turn your movie on and play it anytime and anywhere you wish, as often as you like, and endlessly replay your favorite scenes. The more you play your vision movie consciously over and over in your mind, the more real your movie will become within your subconscious mind. The more real it is within your subconscious mind, the more your vision will automatically manifest itself and become real in your physical world.

By consciously clarifying your vision, you begin to create the life and the world you desire. Although it is in your mind, this is where your aspirations take their first visible form. It is from there that they begin to take shape and substance. Create your vision first in your mind, commit yourself to achieving it, and it will be created in the real world. It will happen because the more you play your vision over and over, the less your mind will distinguish between what you imagine as your vision and what is physical reality. In other words, as far as your mind is concerned, your vision is real. By playing it over and watching it in your mind, your vision becomes real to your mind in the same way that a material object is real to you in the physical world.

To make your vision more powerful, make it very, very clear. Make it as clear as you possibly can. The greater the detail, the greater the clarity, the greater the power of your vision and the more likely it is to transform into reality. For example, to help develop a vision of your life ten years from now, imagine exactly what a typical day for you in ten years time will be like, starting from the moment you wake up until you go to sleep at day's end. Picture it. Be able to describe the full day in words 'hour-by-hour' in as much detail as possible. Only you can imagine and describe what you envision. Only you can create and live your future, so imagine what really matters to you.

Expand your paradigms

Paradigms are the way you either knowingly or unknowingly think about or see things. The paradigms you use are important for solving problems, identifying opportunities and making decisions, because your paradigms either limit or expand your ability to solve problems, and to either grasp or miss new opportunities. It is a question of how you think about, evaluate and see things. Learning to do that in different ways has the potential to make an enormous difference to yourself, your teams and your organization.

The majority of people habitually look at problems and opportunities in particular ways (for example, a limiting paradigm is to see problems as problems rather than opportunities!). The next time a similar problem (opportunity) presents itself, their natural inclination is to look at it through the same paradigms they have always used before. If you do that for any given situation or issue you will arrive at a similar answer to the one you arrived at previously. Since your established paradigms shape your response, unless you acquire and use new paradigms then you cannot realistically expect to look at any problem (opportunity) differently and come up with a different answer or solution. It becomes a concern when the solution you used previously is out of date, or is not as effective or appropriate as it was before. In an ever changing world, that can be a recipe for oblivion in your career, business and organization.

If you aspire to something better than and different from where you are now and your current situation, learn to use different paradigms. It is vital to look beyond the familiar and the obvious since what is familiar and obvious is what most people see and use. Look also beyond what you have used previously in order to avoid arriving at the same old answers and results. By using new paradigms you will discover new perspectives, new solutions and new opportunities, that were always there but not previously apparent to you.

A key point to remember when expanding your paradigms and using new paradigms is that you do not need to give up your existing paradigms. There is frequently some benefit in retaining your previous paradigms so keep them and use them to the extent that they are helpful, but do not rely upon them exclusively. Just keep building your repertoire of paradigms so you can expand your options.

Situational paradigms

We become predictable when we consistently use the same paradigms for similar situations. New paradigms are developed by changing the way we see things, changing the frames of reference we use, and learning to shift our thinking outside the proverbial box.

Shift away from the predictable

Absolute Leaders achieve the extraordinary by using different paradigms to consider situations and problems.

Realize that the paradigms that have worked for you until now might not serve you well in the future if they are what you mainly rely upon. Like most people, you very likely see things only through the filters of your own experience and knowledge base, but you may neither see things as they are intended to be seen, nor hear what is actually said.

Changing and expanding your range of paradigms will help you to see and appreciate things in different ways, to arrive at innovative solutions and find opportunities in what may otherwise seem like insurmountable problems. By doing so, you will acquire new knowledge, experience and wisdom previously inaccessible to you.

Frames of reference

One of our limitations is that we see only the things that we look for because they are the things that are on our mental radar screen or within our frame of reference. Due to our paradigms, we do not see the things that we do not look for even though they may literally be staring us in the face. We frequently cannot see what is obvious to others, so often we need someone else, such as an executive coach or mentor, to point them out to us.

The things that we are familiar with are the easiest things to notice, while the things we are unfamiliar with are much harder to notice so we frequently do not see them at all. Often we do not even know the unfamiliar exist for no other reason than our unfamiliarity with them. They are outside our frame of reference or radar, which makes it very hard to spot them. We are all 'familiar with the familiar' and 'unfamiliar with the unfamiliar'. Therefore, we keep looking at matters in much the same way that we have always looked at them previously. That leads us to keep doing things the same way we have always done and at best achieving the previous, but not better, results.

Familiarity is also one reason why people do not believe they can achieve different results. It is little wonder that so many people hit a ceiling in work or life that they do not realize they can actually break through.

Change your view

One way to think of paradigms is to consider them as analogous to camera lenses that we can use to make movies or take photographs. If we use a zoom lens, we only see a little, as though we had blinkers on. If we use a wide-angle lens, we see far wider and get a much broader perspective. Using a zoom-in lens we see a very narrow spectrum in greater detail because our field of vision is restricted. That can be very helpful, especially when we need to zero-in to focus upon a particular issue and drill down into the detail. However, this is also what often happens when we find ourselves caught up in the 'thick of things', where we cannot see the proverbial forest for the trees. The zoom lens approach limits our vision since it restricts our ability to look for and see a wider perspective. It is after we zoom-out to see the wider perspective, with so many more possibilities available to us to choose from, that we can decide which items we want to zoom-in to focus upon. In short, we need two lenses, a wide-angle lens as well as a zoom lens. Using both lenses allows us to see things from different perspectives, to be flexible in the way we look at things, and to put matters into context

Your perception is your reality

The associations we attach to both people and things affect our perceptions. By changing your associations you will change your perceptions.

How perception works

Perception is what people, through their own personal interpretations, come to believe about someone or something. For any individual, how that person perceives anything or anybody is that individual's reality of that thing or person. This is because the highly subjective nature of personal perceptions makes them real to the individuals who hold them.

Our perceptions are unique to each of us, since we see and interpret things in the context of our own unique knowledge and experience. As a result, we alone define how we perceive anything or anyone. To change our perceptions, we do not need to concentrate upon changing things, events or other people, but instead it requires us to change how we personally arrive at the conclusions that shape our perceptions. The answer to changing our perceptions lies within each of us.

Our perceptions are shaped by whatever we associate with something or someone. If we believe and associate a particular characteristic with a certain person, we will look at that person through the filter of that characteristic. The more we look for it, the more likely we are to find the particular characteristic in order to validate our original opinion of that person, which in turn makes us feel reassured with ourselves, as reflected by such statements like, "See, I just knew he would do that!" For example, if we associate controlling other people with achieving outcomes at work, our initial perception of how to deal with others in the workplace will be to 'control' them because we believe that is necessary to get results. It is a perception that we will hold onto even if it is brought into question by the actions of others and events around us that contradict our perception. It will take a considerable amount of proof to the contrary for us to believe that controlling others will not help us achieve results.

Until we are proven otherwise we are unlikely to even consider changing our perceptions, let alone actually initiating the changes necessary to do so.

Even if we accept logical, contradictory proof to any one of our perceptions, we still need to overcome our emotional attachment and familiarity with holding onto that perception. Only by doing that can we subsequently change our actions and produce a different outcome. In circumstances where the evidence in front of us is contrary to what we perceive and believe, it is essential to change our perceptions if we are to personally evolve, develop and progress. Therefore, the critical issue is how we can change our strongly held perceptions.

The power of association

Since we associate certain things and people with certain characteristics, to change our perceptions we need to form different associations with them. To change your perception about something or someone can only happen by acquiring some new knowledge or new experience that changes the associations you make and your interpretation of those associations. Otherwise, you will maintain the same, previous perceptions and interpretations, carrying on as you did before. If you seek some new knowledge or new experience to change your associations and interpretations then you are far more likely to change your perception.

Since your perceptions are your individual reality, they also affect your interpersonal behavior. The perception you have of someone will affect how you interact with that person. If you perceive him or her positively, then you are likely to interact positively and he or she is also more likely to react positively to your interactions with him. If you perceive that person negatively then negative interactions between him and you are far more likely. By holding a negative perception of the other person, you will tend to act (usually subconsciously) negatively towards that person and he will usually respond to you in the same way. The negative vibrations you send bounce back to you. It is a classic case of getting back what you give, so be mindful that in sending negative vibrations you may get back much more than you contemplated initially.

So how do you change your associations? Learning to associate something positive with something negative can transform a negative association into a positive association. Associating something negative with something positive will change a positive association into a negative association. It depends entirely upon how you look at it. If you look for the negative association you will most likely find it, and therefore form a negative perception. Likewise, if you look for the positive association you will most likely form a positive perception.

Powerful motivation comes from within

Understanding our higher purpose is fundamental to intrinsic motivation as it drives us to do what we do.

Link your career to your higher purpose

The career sub-domain is connected to the other five major sub-domains of life, namely finance, relationships, social, health and spirituality. Some people derive their greatest personal motivation simply from a desire to excel in their chosen career, since they just want to be the best at what they do or perhaps gain recognition as being at the forefront of their chosen industry. They see their life purpose predominantly in their work or career. Others do not.

For many people, their highest life purpose is not in their work or careers, but alternatively in the personal, social or spiritual domains of life. The building of a successful career, can however, allow them to achieve what they aspire to in those other private domains. In that way, developing a successful career or business becomes a means to an end (rather than an end in itself) enabling them to fulfill aspirations and goals in their private lives that otherwise would not be possible.

For example, some people aspire to help others as a higher life purpose and do that through being philanthropic by donating personal time or money (or both) to charity. However, if they are not in a 'time rich' or financial position to do so they cannot accomplish their higher purpose to the extent that they may wish. By developing a successful career or business, they can potentially generate sufficient income and free time to allow them to fulfill their charitable goals. In that way, their community aspirations become a driving motivator for their work or career aspirations.

Intrinsic motivation

By being self-motivated from within and driven by personal meaning, your chances of success will be far greater than if you rely upon external events and other people for motivation. Internal motivation from within comes from the authentic you, as it is based upon what has genuine personal meaning for you. In that context, what is meaningful to you may not necessarily be meaningful to others.

Internal motivation and purpose is a key to Absolute Leadership, since it has more personal relevance than externally based motivation and it increases your interest, self-confidence and energy level. This in turn can create higher levels of persistence to take the necessary actions to achieve your aspirations, thereby leading you to higher levels of self-satisfaction and performance. Other individuals could have a similar degree of competency as you for a particular activity or role, but if you are more highly motivated from within than they are then your performance level will be commensurately higher. That happens because you will apply yourself more diligently, thereby outperforming others with similar potential or competency levels.

The path to becoming an Absolute Leader is a practical example of this notion. If you are motivated from within to lead others, then it is more likely that you will in fact do the reading, attend the leadership courses, get expert coaching, and put into practice what you learn about leadership. By those means you can provide better leadership than others who have a lesser degree of motivation, but that may initially be equally competent to you in leadership ability. Eventually your efforts to develop your leadership competencies will help you to surpass them.

COMPETENCY 2
Adapt to prosper

"Insanity is to keep doing what you have always done and expect a better result!"

Proverb

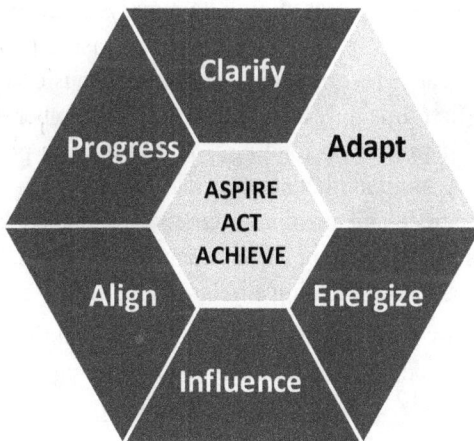

The influence of time

You are the manifestation of your past and your future. The influence of every thought you have ever had, of every action you have ever taken, of every relationship you have ever had, of every experience and of everything that has ever happened to you, is all reflected in who you are now and by your present situation.

In addition to your past, more than you might imagine, you are also the result of what you aspire to and expect for your future. Even though your future has not yet 'happened' in the physical world around you, your expectation of it (whether or not you are aware of what you expect in the future) is already real to your subconscious mind. Through your subconscious mind, your expectations of your future are already having a profound impact upon you, being reflected in what you currently do and the decisions that you make which in turn determine your future. Both your past experiences and your future expectations influence what you do in the present, day-to-day, moment-to-moment.

Past focus

If your focus is predominantly upon your past, then how you live your life and conduct yourself in the present will be mainly influenced by the events of your past. You often hear the influence of the past in people's conversations when they hear a favorite song or piece of music. The music takes them back to the first time they heard it and they remember everything from that moment that happened so long ago. They associate people and events with the music. A similar phenomenon can occur when someone walks down a familiar street and memories come flooding back from walking down that same street or 'memory lane' many years before. Almost certainly you have experienced something similar yourself.

With so many strongly emotional long-term memories stored in people's minds that can be easily recalled by a simple trigger such as a familiar sound or familiar place, it is little wonder that people are often said to 'live in the past'. Such people are said to be nostalgic. They intentionally or unintentionally allow the past to be their major focus and reference point so it becomes the major influence as to how they presently live their lives.

Professionally, something similar happens when individuals talk about what they did in a previous career, business or organization. Talking about it excessively often indicates a strong orientation in their past. The stronger they are oriented in their past, the more they are apt to repeat the past and the experiences that they had in a previous occupation or situation. It may be beneficial if the aim is to copy or clone another organization, but that is seldom if ever the case.

In some instances, there can be some merit in a strong orientation in the past where it provides helpful learning for the present and the future. For example, people that have been with a business or organization for a long time often have what is called 'organizational history'. These people tend to know why things are done the particular way they are done in an organization and they are very familiar with the historical culture of an organization because they have lived, survived and frequently prospered by being part of that history and culture. Such people bring the advantages of organizational continuity that includes knowing how an organization has functioned up to the present time. They know what has worked and what has not worked. They possess and are part of organizational wisdom. These people are often very loyal and they have almost always adapted themselves extremely well within the organization, and in many cases have been able to influence the organization to adapt to them in some way. You most likely know some people who fit that description. Collectively, such people can either be a major hurdle for an organization to implement change, or they can provide a useful base for some stable continuity.

Future focus

People with a strong future focus are often so busy devising new ideas and strategies for the future that they are likely to avoid dealing with what is actually happening in the present. They frequently fail to link present actions to the future because they often do not appreciate the practical link between the present and the future, namely that actions in the present bring about the future. Even if they see the link between the present and the future, they may still fail to take the required actions in the present necessary to create their desired future.

If you constantly talk about your dreams and your conversations constantly reflect wonderful dreams or visions, but you do not take the actions necessary to turn your dreams into reality, then the label of 'dreamer' most probably applies to you. It is essential to have dreams and vision, but it is rather pointless living only in dreamland. The objective is to live out and experience your aspirational dreams in the real world and that requires conscious, deliberate mental and physical effort. The dreams and visions that you imagine will come true only through taking action, which is the second 'A' or principle of Absolute Leadership.

Present focus

If you are focused predominantly in the present then you operate mainly in the doing or action realm, rather than in the realms of thinking or dreaming. However, being overly oriented in the present can mean that you are so busy that you do not see the bigger picture. You might not see the proverbial forest for the trees. You may only be using a zoom lens, not a wide-angle lens. You might also not be able to imagine or see the future, and like someone oriented in the past you might unfortunately be inclined to dismiss taking strategic actions such as imagining your future and business planning, thereby denying yourself a better career and life. You run the risk of limiting your advancement to a higher level, by repeating, year in and year out, what you have always done and currently still do.

Be grateful

Absolute Leaders are grateful for everything that has happened to them, good or bad. This includes being grateful for when things go well, and also for when matters do not go how they like or according to plan. The probability is that there will always be some of what we do that does not turn out how we would have preferred at the time. There are beneficial lessons in even the worst things that happen to us despite the obscurity at the time of what those benefits might be. We do ourselves a helpful service to look for and comprehend the learning in our experiences, to be thankful for the lessons, and to move on.

As strange as it may seem to some people, in a similar way we can also be grateful for what has not yet happened to us. Taking obstacles as an example, it is unrealistic to expect that we will not come up against both foreseen and unforeseen obstacles in seeking our future and achieving our aspirations. As much as we may not like obstacles, they do serve a purpose even if we are unaware of their exact benefits at the time we encounter them. Likewise, we must expect that many good things will happen to us along the way, even if they do not happen as we anticipate in the manner we initially hope, expect or plan for them to happen. Of course, many events and people that will come into our lives will be totally unexpected and welcomed. The bottom line is that whether we perceive it as good or bad at the time, and irrespective of who does or does not come into our lives, or what happens or does not happen, we can be thankful for everything even before it actually happens.

No regrets

People often say that they wish they could have changed something they did in the past, or not have done something that they actually did. That type of regretful thinking is futile because what has happened in the past cannot be changed. There is no going back to undo and redo. Absolute Leaders realize there is no winding back of the clock (other than in someone's memory). Every single moment in the past has gone never to return. You can repeatedly replay past moments and events in your mind through your memories, but that will only get you stuck back where you were to begin with. The futility of it is that when people are caught up in the past they fail to live fully in the present, and they obstruct themselves from bringing into existence a better future for themselves and others.

Examples of regret abound in individuals' careers and private lives. They are exemplified by comments that begin with "If only..." such as, "If only I had done that instead of this", "If only I had gone there instead of stayed here", and "If only I had chosen a profession other than the one I did". The list of potential "If only..." statements is endless. Absolute Leaders realize that 'what is done, is done' so they do not live in an "If only..." world.

Realize that the only change you can ever make is in the present, and it is only through your actions in the present that you will ever build your future. Moreover, you can only make the present different from the past if you are clear about your future and are prepared to do whatever is necessary to create a future for yourself that is more rewarding than your past. The answer to dealing with any feelings of regret is not to repeat the actions that caused them in the first place. Move on without regret!

The nature of expectations

Expectations influence the very actions needed for them to materialize. The manner in which people do something is largely determined by what they expect the outcomes to be. Aspirations and expectations are not the same thing. Many people aspire to something but do not particularly expect it will materialize.

Expect positive outcomes

Expectations are self-fulfilling prophecies. Whatever your expectations are, they influence your actions, and subsequently they influence your situation and outcomes because your actions and behaviors are oriented towards your expectations. You will far more likely get what you expect rather than what you do not expect. Your actions and performance will almost certainly match whatever your own expectations are as regards your life and career outcomes.

From a workplace perspective, even when overall business conditions are difficult or your organization is in upheaval, your minimum expectation should be to maintain your relative competitive position from a career, business or organizational perspective. In other words, at a minimum expect to keep abreast of any changes in order to keep your job or sustain your business. If you expect to maintain or improve your position irrespective of what is happening around you, there is a much greater chance that you actually will. This is one reason why Absolute Leaders perform better than others during challenging or turbulent times. In the very least, they do not expect to fall professionally behind in comparison to others. They are more optimistic and they expect that there will be possibilities and opportunities to advance themselves, their teams and organizations, through any organizational turmoil, or economic, political, social, and technological challenges.

Clearly, whatever you expect will affect your outlook. By changing your expectations either positively or negatively, your results will change either up or down correspondingly. The key is to always maintain positive expectations regarding your actions and your results. If you expect that your aspirations will, in fact, happen, then they most likely will.

Expect positive actions

To transform your expectations into reality, actively work on clarifying them as well as work towards them. You must actually do something about your expectations by taking appropriate actions; if not, the chances are very remote of your expectations ever becoming reality.

When taking actions, Absolute Leaders do so with the expectation that the actions they take will in fact produce the expected outcomes. Otherwise why take the actions in the first place? However, when some individuals do things they do not actually expect anything in particular to come of what they do. Their expectation (or rather the lack of it) in turn affects how they act, which is how self-fulfilling prophecies become perpetuated. The key is to have deliberate, specific and positive expectations when you act, thereby facilitating the fulfillment of your expectations. You must also learn and acquire the expertise necessary in the form of new skills, knowledge, wisdom and intuition. Often that can be achieved through personal learning, whilst at other times it requires finding and engaging other people who already have the requisite knowledge and skills needed to help you accomplish something.

Self-belief

The ability to do anything competently is determined by your self-belief that you will be able to do so. Self-belief is fundamental to personal development and also serves as a great inspiration for others.

Self-belief and action

Self-belief is self-motivating and ultimately leads to self-fulfillment. The level of your self-belief makes an enormous difference to your actions and ultimately to your achievements and overall quality of life. If you believe that you are capable of doing something, you will most likely take the actions necessary to do it, and perform in a capable and confident manner. However, if you do not believe you are capable, you are unlikely to take even the first step. Even if you do take the first step you could still substantially diminish your chances of performing well, simply because you erroneously allow yourself to think you cannot really do it or cannot do it very well. Therefore, if you think and believe that you can do something competently, there is every chance that in fact you will.

It follows that if you believe you can overcome challenges and obstacles as they occur, then you will most likely overcome them. By contrast, if you believe the challenges you face are insurmountable then you are less likely to seek and develop the means to overcome them, making it almost impossible to do so. The fact is that you can do anything you really want to and of which you are also capable, but whether you actually do it will be affected by your self-belief.

Use your self-belief to inspire others

Believe in yourself and you will find it far easier to inspire other people to also believe in you, and in what you do. People will be disinclined to believe in you if they perceive that you have no belief in your own capabilities. They may say that they believe in you, they may empathize with you, and they may even sympathize with you. Nonetheless, despite what they say, and regardless of their empathy or sympathy, they will not believe in you if you do not demonstrate your own self-belief.

Furthermore, through your own self-belief, you can inspire others to believe in themselves and develop their own self-belief. Absolute Leaders do this and it is one way they build support teams and create willing followers. When other people see that you, as a leader, have self-belief, they will often look at you as a role model or somebody that they admire, and they will be inspired to follow your lead and develop greater self-belief in their own lives and careers. In essence, they learn how to improve their own self-belief from what they learn through observing you as their leader and role model.

How to see opportunities

If you look for problems you will tend to find problems. Equally, if you look for opportunities you will tend to find opportunities. One way to change problem oriented thinking is to change your expectations from finding problems to finding opportunities. Expect to see opportunities rather than problems and you will indeed see and find opportunities. One way to find opportunities is by using reverse engineering. The process is to consider what you would like the outcome of a situation to be, then search for a step-by-step solution to achieve the outcome. The most important step will be the first one. Once you see and take that, the rest will follow.

Two shoe salespeople travel to a new area where their company has not previously sold shoes. When they arrive they notice that no-one wears shoes. The first salesperson calls his manager and tells him there is a big problem since nobody wears shoes, so he is catching the first plane back home. The second salesperson calls the same manager and asks him to urgently send plenty of stock because there is a huge opportunity!

Go beyond self-limiting myths

Myths are beliefs that we assume, or like to believe, are true, but they are either not true or not true in all situations. If we assume that they are always true, they limit us because we fail to adapt ourselves as circumstances and situations change, or we fail to take the necessary actions to better direct our future. Some of the most limiting myths are those to do with success, education and experience.

Previous success

Previous success can limit individuals through not appreciating the influence of organizational situations and using previous success to defend current performance.

Organizational context

Another reason success can be a barrier is because skills and competencies need to suit the requirements of an organization's developmental stage. Take, for example, an executive who excels within an organization that has just gone through recent dramatic growth. During high business growth stages, the development of systems and processes frequently lag behind. After growth, the next stage of development is usually consolidation, during which the systems and processes in the organization catch up to the previous business growth. This plateau of activity might not suit the executive whose skills are better matched to high growth or start-up businesses. It can lead to a mismatch since what was required during the growth stage is less suitable during the consolidation stage. Yet many individuals fail to adapt to new circumstances, not realizing what worked for them before simply does not work anywhere near as well because of the changed situational context. They then begin to flounder and underperform if they do not take the necessary actions to learn new behaviors and adapt themselves.

Success as a defense

Sometimes, previous success leads individuals to rest on their laurels. They want to be judged by their earlier success or track record, but what really matters at any moment is how well they currently perform in their present role. Frequently, they use previous success as a barrier to defend themselves against shortcomings in their current performance, when what they really need to do is prove the value they presently add to an organization through their current role or actions. As an Absolute Leader, however much you may be proud of your earlier achievements, do not rest upon them. You can only add value to your teams, businesses and organizations, through your present activities, and you should be able to clearly articulate how you intend to add value in the future.

Formal education

Relevant formal education is a base line requirement for most occupations and job roles because people simply cannot satisfactorily perform in a role if they do not have the prerequisite training. However, what formal education and training does not provide is that which is learnt through workplace experience, called experiential learning or experiential knowledge. Some people may consider formal education a substitute for learning from experience, but that is erroneous.

When employers recruit individuals, educational achievements indicate commitment, discipline, and intellect by the applicant. Completing an educational or training qualification sends a positive message to an employer because it demonstrates individual commitment and achievement. What education and training does not prove is that the individual can actually perform in a particular role. It does not prove workplace competence, nor does it prove that the individual can get along with other people in a workplace environment.

Formal education trains you to develop certain ways of approaching and doing things that can determine the skill set you bring into a role or situation. Certain skills are generally associated with certain professions because of the training provided. Amongst other skills, lawyers train to look for issues, accountants train to crunch numbers, engineers train to solve problems, and marketers train to persuade consumers. The tools of each trade or profession are different. If the skills associated with your particular profession or training become the dominant way you look at organizational, business and people issues, then that will affect the way you conduct yourself in your interactions with others. In brief, what you learn or have learnt through your formal education can limit you when alternative skills and paradigms would be unquestionably more beneficial to your professional or leadership development.

Many individuals I coach are very well educated. Frequently, one of their initial comments is that they believe they have little to gain from leadership or executive coaching because they are so well educated. They want to know what coaching can 'teach' them. Although teaching and learning are clearly connected, they are definitely not the same thing. The aim of coaching is not particularly to teach someone, but more importantly for the person being coached to 'learn'. When they realize that coaching focuses upon enabling their own learning to develop and perform to a higher level, it highlights the fact that their own education, or the experience of how they have been educated, in fact narrows rather than broadens their outlook, their learning and their success.

Repeated experience

You could have many years of experience but all you might be doing is repeating the same thing 'day-in, day-out' and 'year-in, year-out'. What you end up with is not many years of experience, but rather one year of experience repeated many times over.

Frequently I come across individuals who have been in the same role for many years. Some ask the question, "I have been doing this for twenty years, so I do not see how you could help me?" When we then delve deeper into their question (the question itself sometimes being a good indicator of their attitude to self-improvement), it frequently turns out that they have been doing the same things (more or less) for numerous years and that they have also been doing those same things the same way (more or less) for all those years. They may well be proficient at what they repeat everyday, they may have even become masters of what they repeatedly do, but they have not grown professionally or developed to their full capability. Far from it! They confuse their numerous years of experience with the fact that, in the worst cases, they really have only one year of experience repeated countless times over! They really have not progressed far if at all, but because they have 'experience', they delude themselves into equating years of experience in a certain role with mastery or competency of that role. They could not be more mistaken and their own 'extensive' experience inhibits them from fulfilling their true potential, experiencing something far more rewarding, and satisfying.

When people keep doing what they have been doing the same way and they keep repeating the same experiences, it is because they wish to remain their comfort zone. It is what they know. The people that resist changing, who seek to cocoon themselves inside their comfort zone when it is best to change, can be inclined to try to manipulate the world and situations around them so that they do not have to adapt how they think and what they do. They try to make the world and others adapt to them, instead of trying to be flexible by adapting to the world and other people. Ultimately, their strategy either fails completely or it produces results far inferior to what otherwise could have been achieved.

While experiencing the same thing over and over again might result in them feeling good, it often costs them and their organizations money because they are not making real progress! The critical issue is not how many years experience, but how much progress they have made over that time. How has their performance and competency improved with experience over time? Sometimes their response to that question is a very uncomfortable silence. Yet when they engage in leadership development and commit to pursue their full potential by actually learning from their experiences, things begin to change for the better. Almost without exception, they produce remarkable transformations in themselves (and others) over relatively short timeframes. The benefits are often enormous, far exceeding expectations.

Absolute Leaders are always able to identify a range of new skills and knowledge that they have learnt and applied in their area of expertise. If you have been in a role for many years but have not learnt or grown a great deal in that role, then for all the years in your role your actual experience could in reality be quite limited. Therefore, the value of your experience is also limited. You may have stuck too long with what you already know and more than likely you do not know what would be helpful for you, because you have blinkers on. If that sounds like you, take your blinkers off by changing your paradigms, seizing the opportunities to learn new skills, creating greater value, and making substantially more progress through your experience!

Brick walls

A brick wall is something or someone that stops your progress towards achieving your aspirations or goals. Most people come up against a brick wall at some point during their lives. A common tendency, when confronted with a brick wall that someone wants to get past, is to try to quickly find a way to get beyond it. The obvious options are: to scale over it; or to make a hole big enough in the brick wall to go through it; or to find the end of the wall and go around it; or to burrow a hole to crawl under it; or, to find a way to pull the brick wall down and walk over the rubble.

All these approaches can work and they all require energy, but a crucial issue to answer, firstly, is whether getting past the brick wall is worth the energy. The only way you can decide that is to find out what is on the other side of the brick wall. Do that before you try to get past the wall to avoid potentially wasting a lot of time and energy.

Talents, strengths and weaknesses

Use your natural talents, but do not rely exclusively upon them. Be sure to turn your strengths into talents, and address your weakness.

Natural talents

Talents are gifts that you are born with. Everyone has gifts, and lucky are those who discover them sooner rather than later. However, natural talent on its own is not enough for exceptional achievement. Instead, talent is often a major cause of complacency since many people erroneously believe that because they are naturally talented at something they do not have to work at it to succeed.

Irrespective of differences in talent between individuals, people who work relentlessly and diligently at what they do will inevitably succeed more than people who do not. Lesser talented individuals do not necessarily become more talented than the more gifted (although that does happen), but they inevitably achieve more and derive greater satisfaction. In a sense they become more 'talented at achieving' rather than being simply 'talented'. That usually gives lesser naturally talented individuals who apply themselves a defining, competitive edge.

If you do not work at developing your natural talent, then someone with equal or lesser talent who works harder can easily surpass you, something you can rest assured will happen in any competitive environment. Do not be surprised if that has already happened to you, as you have plenty of highly talented companions in the same situation! Others who are less naturally talented than you can develop alternative strengths that more than compensate for any gap in natural talent between you and them. Even with a relatively large talent gap, they too can leave you in their wake if you are a highly talented but 'lazy' individual.

People with natural talents are frequently used to getting ahead merely by relying upon their talents. Initially that is often effective, but eventually the advantage of natural talent by its own is not enough to sustain a competitive edge. Those who are naturally talented expect to succeed relying solely upon their raw talent, without necessarily improving it further. As a consequence, they do not apply themselves as well as they could, which opens the door of opportunity for someone with less natural talent to outperform them.

The way to compensate for a lesser talent is to improve whatever talents you have, and to develop other strengths by regularly, relentlessly, and diligently practicing them. There is no alternative. It is what less naturally talented (but not less successful) people do to win and succeed against people with greater natural talent. Although a winning edge is not guaranteed, they will have a good chance of beating those who are more naturally gifted at their own game. The possibility of doing that is highly motivating so they consistently work away at developing their skills competency.

Two examples of natural talents include the ability to recognize numerical patterns and having the 'gift of the gab'. The individual with numerical talent can quickly spot number patterns that most people cannot identify, and likewise the gifted speaker can persuade others through talk. While both the mathematician and the speaker can do what they do without a great deal of effort, just as if they were pre-programmed or operating on autopilot, consider how they could potentially improve the benefit of their natural talents. The individual with an eye for numerical patterns may benefit by learning to decipher more critical (numerical) information from less critical information, separating the proverbial 'grain from the chaff'. Similarly, for the person with the gift of the gab, learning to actively listen thereby allowing other people to have their say can make that person a more effective communicator.

The bottom line is to know your talents, develop them as much as possible so you use them to your advantage, but also to develop other skills that allow you to use your talents better.

Build your strengths

A strength is something you do well, but that is not a gift. It is something that comes relatively easy to you but not as automatic as a natural talent. A strength gives you advantage, it is something you enjoy doing, and it gives you a sense of satisfaction.

Your strengths can fluctuate in their power and usefulness according to how well you develop and use them. The adage 'Use it or lose it" applies, as is the case with natural talent. Using and building your strengths is one of the most important things to do as an Absolute Leader. People generally have far more strengths than talents, so there are usually several strengths at least that people can work on and develop. The key is to identify the strengths that are most beneficial to you and that you enjoy most, and then focus on developing each one of those strengths to the best of your ability. By doing so, you will have an array of competent strengths that you will enjoy using to help you progress towards your aspirational aims.

Address your weaknesses

Absolute Leaders address their weaknesses, because a single, yet critical weakness that is not resolved can stall a person's progress. Many people believe that they cannot fix or should not fix their weaknesses, but rather they ought to somehow just live with them and concentrate entirely upon their talents and strengths. Their approach is to utilize talents, build strengths, and ignore weaknesses. If weaknesses are not addressed they can become major barriers to your career advancement as well as affect your personal life. You cannot ignore your weaknesses, since they can stop you from achieving your aspirations. Address your weaknesses, compensate for them, and learn to manage them, so that they do not limit you.

Decision making

In the decision making hierarchy of Absolute Leadership there are five different levels of decision making that rank from Information based decision making at the base level, then proceed up to Knowledge, Experience, Wisdom, and finally to Intuition. What really matters is your practical application of the know-how you have at each decision making level, to the decisions you make.

Based upon your know-how and your learning, at any level a decision can still be wrong or be the less appropriate decision. For example, you may arrive at an incorrect conclusion from accurate information, or the wisdom that generally serves you well may need to be re-considered in a different situational context, such as for different cultures within or between organizations or countries. Nonetheless, accepting the risk that your decisions will not always be the best ones to make or will result in unforeseen consequences, is just part of the decision making process.

All of the five decision making levels have a place and serve a purpose, but what sets Absolute Leaders apart from others is their high level abilities, especially in the use of intuition and wisdom, and the higher frequency with which they use those two higher levels of decision making. They also learn from experience quicker than others do (partly because they want to learn and they continually 'learn how to learn'), so they have a higher degree of experiential competency. Their better ability to exercise the higher levels of decision making increases their capacity to adapt to change and powerfully influence other people. Ultimately, it makes them better leaders.

Information

It is often said that 'information is power'. To qualify that statement, information only has the potential for power if the other party does not have the same information. Its value also depends a great deal upon its utility and the skill with which it is used. Having information for information sake alone does not particularly help decision making nor influence other people. One way to manage, control and manipulate others is to withhold information that you have but that they do not, and which would be helpful and therefore be of value to them. Being in charge of the distribution of such information gives you power that is directly proportional to the value or utility of the information.

However, access to information, for example, via the internet, shifts or negates the power of online information (the internet was originally designed for sharing information). Web based information flows in all sorts of directions, and the more people who can access it, the lesser its economic value. The same diminishing value principle applies to information available through any other source.

There is always a risk that too much information can cloud an issue, thereby making it unnecessarily more difficult to arrive at a decision. The greater the amount of available information, the greater the potential risk that some parts of the information will contradict other parts, or least be more prone to be interpreted as contradictory. As more and more information is accumulated, the value of each incremental piece of information becomes increasingly marginal for decision making. As an Absolute Leader, one of the important things to learn is determining when you have enough of the right information to confidently make a decision. If you do not need all the information, or you know when you have enough of it, waiting for any more information will simply procrastinate your decision.

Knowledge

Information in itself without understanding is not knowledge. Information is the base of knowledge, but knowledge is of far greater value than information. Information is based on data (facts and numbers), whereas knowledge is the actual understanding, interpreting, and making sense of data, all of which gives knowledge much more value than information. The greater the ability to understand, interpret and apply knowledge, the greater the value of knowledge and the greater the value of the individual, team or organization that possesses and utilizes the knowledge.

Information provides details about something, but information by itself does not give you knowledge 'to know a subject'; nor give you the ability to ascertain what information is relevant; nor the ability to identify the patterns in information; nor the ability to put information into context to use it for better decision making. However, once you can do all that you are along the path to knowing, or having 'knowledge of the information'. Knowledge, therefore, derives value from its subjective nature.

Experience

The real value or benefit of experience is the lessons learnt from it. As we have already seen, some people learn a great deal from experience whilst others learn very little. Two of the key lessons from experience are, firstly, how to handle unfamiliar situations, and secondly, the development of competency.

One thing experience can do for us is to place us in situations different to those we have encountered before. We are then faced with having to navigate our way and make decisions in unfamiliar circumstances. Some of the decisions we make will serve us well, whilst other decisions we make will not, but whatever we learn about the suitability of our decisions happens only through our experiences in the various situations in which we find ourselves. In that way experience can help us to learn about context.

A second important lesson from experience is competency. Competency largely comes from developing and improving knowledge and skills through practical experience. By applying and practicing your knowledge you develop experience of that knowledge or experiential competency. Likewise with skills, since the more you apply and practice them, the greater the experiential competency you acquire. Progressive people in the workplace develop their knowledge and skills through the experience of practice. That is why professional service businesses are often referred to as 'professional practices', as for example legal practices, medical practices and accounting practices. To develop your leadership skills you must put them into practice, thereby gaining leadership experience through which you acquire leadership competency. To that end, coaching expedites leadership development because it accelerates the practice of leadership competencies by the individuals who are coached.

Wisdom

Wisdom is the conscious and judicious use of knowledge for value or benefit. You create value by how well you apply your knowledge and skills, so hence knowledge and skills normally help to build wisdom but it isn't always so. The accumulation of knowledge helps create wisdom but does not guarantee it. Individuals can have a lot of knowledge and skill but not be very wise.

To develop wisdom, knowledge and skills have to be applied discerningly through your actions, which in turn form your experience. You take actions based upon your knowledge and receive feedback from your actions as to whether they produce the intended results. The feedback is information that you process into knowledge about your actions. In that way it allows you to develop wisdom so that next time you are confronted with a similar situation you can make an appropriate decision about what action to take. By learning through experience, you come to understand in advance the consequences of taking or avoiding specific actions, and also how to undertake actions in a manner that produces the outcomes you seek. In essence, you develop the ability to use your judgment to make wise decisions.

Intuition

Intuition is inherited to help us make decisions for our personal survival. Everyone is born with intuition, using it long before they ever develop logical thinking and reasoning abilities.

The nature of intuition

The world is not all just about facts and logical reasoning. It is also very much to do with intuition. Intuition is very helpful when there is no logical explanation available, or no information, or no precedent knowledge, action, or experience to guide us. Sometimes we have to make decisions in the absence of logical reasoning, which is where intuition can play an especially vital role.

Intuition for many people goes against the grain of their formal education, because through education they are taught to predominantly or exclusively rely upon logic, or upon some type of substantiating evidence, or upon the process of scientific hypothesis testing, in order to prove something is either true or false. Taken to an extreme they learn not to trust their intuition at all, or at least not to act upon their intuition when logic is placed in front of them as an alternative. They learn that logic is the safer option because it allows them to rationalize or justify actions based upon 'data' whereas intuition does not.

As indicated, intuition works by drawing upon our creative and innate abilities to make decisions. The natural tendency of people is to rely upon facts and information (which may be incorrect, irrelevant or incomplete), and they frequently rely upon them so much that when they do not have them they become immobilized. They do not know what to do, so they tend to freeze and do not take action. That causes procrastination since there is a lack of decision making, which in turn can lead to increased stress levels and to missed opportunities for themselves, their teams and organizations. Even when their intuition tells them the decision to make and the actions to take, they fail to follow their intuition because they have not learnt to use it and trust it.

Using intuition

In an organization it can be very difficult to justify what you have done based largely or solely upon intuition, although that depends to some extent upon the type of culture in your organization and the level of power, authority and influence you possess. In most situations you will need hard information, knowledge and the benefit of experience and at least a dose of wisdom to back you up. If you doubt that, just try explaining a major complex decision to your boss based solely upon your intuition!

In some cases, even where there is plenty of quality information, knowledge and experience, the logic and rationale of the case presented can run counter to instinct. It is not uncommon to have a gut (instinctive) feeling that goes against a logical argument or conventional wisdom. We do not necessarily dispute the logic and its conclusions, but the instinct inside us is more powerful and feels more right than the information or argument presented. This often happens where new information is inconsistent with our established experience and expertise. Often we know there is something inconsistent, but we do not know exactly what it is at that point. Therein exists a dilemma for most people, being upon what basis to make a decision. Absolute Leaders overcome that dilemma because they learn to develop their intuition, and the more they develop and use it assists their decision making.

Team and organizational decisions

As well as being applicable to individuals, the decision making hierarchy also applies collectively to teams and organizations. Teams and organizations have collective information, knowledge, experience, wisdom and even intuition, through the people who comprise them, as well as through individuals connected by networks.

In a team and organizational context, components of the various levels of the decision making hierarchy are distributed throughout the member individuals. Different individuals possess different subparts of the total information, knowledge, experience, wisdom and intuition within a team or organization. As well, different individuals will have strengths in particular levels and aspects of the hierarchy. For example, in a team of three people, one team member may have substantial information but little experience; the second team member may have considerable experiential learning, some information and lots of practical knowledge; and the third team member may have much greater wisdom but lesser knowledge and information.

The significant point is that the relative contribution to decision making by each of the three team members will usually enhance the caliber of team decisions. Over time the team develops collectively at every level of the decision making hierarchy, building and developing its own information, knowledge, experience, wisdom and intuition.

The same applies across an organization. The ability of individuals to make decisions at any management level is affected by the strength of an organization's decision making hierarchy. That strength develops over time, but it is also affected either negatively or positively by people joining or leaving the organization. To illustrate, an individual joining an organization or team should preferably enhance the decision hierarchy at one or more of the five levels, thereby improving the overall caliber of organizational decision making; or alternatively, a new recruit could in fact weaken organizational decision making (in which case the wrong person was recruited).

Adapt and change

Everyone has the ability to adapt and change. How people handle change is influenced by their attitude or paradigms towards it. Interestingly, many people fear change because they often see change as a major event rather than as the continual small changes constantly happening around them.

Paradigms of change

Absolute Leaders change and adapt themselves to fulfill their aspirations and goals. At times they adapt as a response to external change or in anticipation of impending change, whilst at other times they simply adapt to be better prepared for their envisioned future. They change and adapt for a variety of reasons, including performance at their utmost best, and to compete at the highest level of their chosen career. They recognize that to stay the way they are is really to allow others to move ahead of them, which means they fall behind. They understand that nothing ever stands still, that everything is dynamic. They develop, improve and adapt themselves to retain a competitive advantage for themselves, their teams, their organizations and their industry. They appreciate that the paradigms they use to look at change can make all the difference, and that while at its most basic level change is about survival, it also about growth and opportunity.

Change is growth

Absolute Leaders understand change as the normal course of the world evolving. The history of civilizations and societies is one of constant change. Look around and you will see change or the results of change everywhere. History teaches us that the world we live in will always continue to change, so to expect that the future will be like the present is simply unrealistic. History demonstrates, over and over again, that changing and adapting is imperative to our survival and prosperity, both individually and collectively. It is through change that we advance our societies, organizations and ourselves, since change impels us to find more effective ways to view things, to find new solutions to old problems, and to meet the challenges of resolving new problems as they occur, in order that we can move forward.

Organizations are like societies or civilizations, characterized by leaders, structures, systems, rules and cultures. They too can rise and fall. In fact, the rise and fall of empires, civilizations, organizations or individuals, has often been brought about by their inability to anticipate, respond appropriately or adapt, to changes.

People that adapt themselves in anticipation of change or as things change around them, will usually prosper. In the very least they will more than likely survive. For those who do not adapt to changes, the best they can hope for is survival but often they will perish.

Consider how you have changed. You are not the same person that you were, say five years ago, or even one year ago. Consider what has changed in your life such as your attitudes, your beliefs, your relationships, and your physical appearance. You may have new friends and acquaintances and have perhaps lost touch with others. What has changed in your career or business? What are you doing now professionally that you did not even contemplate a year ago, let alone five years ago? Whatever you aim to be doing in a year, five years, ten years or twenty years time will most likely be different from what you are doing now, so you will have little option but to adapt yourself as inevitable changes take place.

According to Darwin's theory of evolution, those that survive do so because they adapt. By adapting, they become fitter to survive in their environment, whilst those that fail to adapt ultimately become extinct. Consider that in terms of yourself and your own organization or business. Are you, your business and organization adapting? If so, how well are you adapting? If not, are you on the road to extinction? You need to be making changes and adapting ahead of your competitors and others, so that you survive, prosper and sustain yourself and those around you, far into the future.

Change is opportunity

You cannot take advantage of opportunity presented by change if you are in self-denial that either the change itself or that the potential for opportunity exists.

Move past denial

If you are accustomed to feeling threatened by change, then in all probability you will treat new change as yet another threat and put up all your usual defenses. The first defense to change is denial of the change itself, and the second defense is denying the need to adapt. If that sounds a bit like you then at this point review the paradigms you use to consider change and begin to think outside the square. That will help you move past denial and look at change in a different way.

Look for the benefits

Change compels us to consider things in new ways if we are to benefit. It can make us realize that we need to learn something new and do something new in order to progress. It provides the opportunities for new experiences because of changed circumstances. It allows us to re-assess how we apply our values and beliefs in the context of what is changing. It provides opportunities for us to reconfirm our own self-belief that we can indeed make the most of, and benefit, from any changes.

Change sends clear messages that what has been working for us as individuals and as societies or organizations will no longer work for us. Its use by date is here or it has already passed. It necessitates that we adapt, creating something different and far better suited, or opportunistic, to the new environment that change brings about.

Consider for a moment how making changes and adapting could benefit you. How would you benefit if you implemented some changes? What changes could you make? Visualize those changes and imagine how you would benefit from them. Consider how your teams, networks and organization would benefit. Within change exist opportunities for you and those with whom you interact to benefit. Instead of resisting and fighting the changes, you can gain much more by accepting, embracing and exploiting them to work for you.

Creators, embracers and laggards

In consumer behavior, it is estimated that about three percent of people are innovators or initiators of change, about twelve percent are early adopters or early embracers, and the remaining eighty-five percent are the laggards that reluctantly but eventually succumb to change.

The creators or initiators of change take the greatest degree of risk, but they also stand to reap the greatest potential benefits since they are the ones that move off the mark first. They are often also the people who tend to closely monitor developments and trends in their profession and industry. Those that follow quickly afterwards, the embracers, adopt change because they realize the benefits of the changes implemented and adopted by the initiators. Embracers also include opinion leaders who help shape the actions of others. Early embracers take a moderate amount of risk because the change or innovation may not be totally proven. Yet they realize that it is probably much more beneficial to adopt change and adapt, rather than run the potentially much greater risk of being left so far behind that they may never catch up.

The last group, the laggards, are the ones that follow the crowd. They can be divided into two sub-groups. The first sub-group, are those with a herd mentality who either realize the inevitability of change but they do not want to miss out so they follow, or they are strongly influenced by the opinion leaders in the embracers group. The second sub-group never really accept change wholeheartedly (or even half-heartedly), but with the only other option being to opt out completely (a few sometimes do this), they have little choice but to inevitably go along with everyone else. By the time they do that, the first group, the initiators, has moved onto something altogether new, so the laggards never catch up!

Paradoxes of change

Paradoxes of change include notions of uncertainty versus certainty, and the unfamiliar versus continuity of the familiar.

Change, uncertainty and security

A major issue in dealing with change for most people concerns what they associate with change. Firstly, many people associate change with uncertainty and they associate uncertainty with insecurity. Hence, they conclude that change is insecurity.

A second and alternative approach is to associate change with certainty, in the sense that change is constantly happening whether we like or not, so it is absurd to deny that fact. Change is a constant. Since constant change is a certainty, and certainty results in security, then change is in fact security!

It is clear from the two viewpoints of change just described that the argument for arriving at either conclusion, that change is either insecurity or security, is constructed in the same way. What changes the conclusion reached is the association that people make with change. The choice of associating either security or insecurity with change is what makes the difference, and choosing that association is up to the individual. In your own life and circumstances it is up to you. The choice made by Absolute Leaders is to associate change with security, not insecurity.

Change, continuity and comfort zones

Adapting and changing seldom requires discarding everything we have or had before. Depending upon the degree of change and the long-term objectives, continuity can have very significant value. We look for and like continuity because we are often happier to keep things as they are. We want the reassurance of what we know and are familiar with, rather than what is new and unfamiliar. Continuity gives some people a link back to times of comfort thereby keeping them in their comfort zone.

You might have noticed that people often fondly look back to times when circumstances were hard. Even though they might not have liked what was happening back then, they recall those times with great affection. Since they directly experienced those times, they are comfortable with them because those times are 'known' and familiar. They are comfort zones. An example is the global financial crisis. As despairing and testing it has been for many people, many will look back at it in later years with great affection and warmth because their personal experience will have made it known and familiar to them, etching it into their emotional psyche. Today's crisis is tomorrow's comfort!

The magnitude of change

Changes can be categorized according to their magnitude as; (i) Incremental; (ii) Transformational; and (iii) Reinvention.

Incremental changes

Incremental changes are usually, and perhaps surprisingly, the greatest potential challenge because we often do not even notice them although they frequently happen. Since they are small changes occurring just 'one small change at a time', we often do not become too concerned about them until the cumulative effect becomes apparent.

The biggest potential threat

The size of each incremental change is usually too small of itself to be of major concern to us. Frequently we may not even notice the change, or if we do, we may not feel threatened nor perceive a need to respond because each small change has no 'shock' value. The shock value only comes later as an accumulated impact when we eventually realize what had been slowly building up all along right under our noses, but we were not sufficiently alert or astute enough to detect the changes.

In a famous experiment on reaction to change, a frog was placed in a jar of boiling water. The frog immediately reacted by struggling desperately to escape from the jar but it could not. It boiled to death. Another frog was placed in a jar of cool water that was then heated very, very slowly. As the water temperature slowly increased, the frog made no attempt to escape and eventually it too boiled to death. However, the second frog did not notice the change in water temperature because the change was very, very slow. The change was incremental, but nonetheless it still caused the frog's demise, because the frog did not detect the subtle temperature changes and therefore did not react to jump out of the jar and save itself.

There is a lesson to be learnt from the frog experiments. We must be aware of the changes in all facets of our environment and monitor even the smallest, consistent changes, because, over time, they can have a major cumulative impact and threaten our very existence. The small, cumulative, incremental type changes that go unnoticed are often the biggest threat. When we ignore them it is at our own peril.

Applying the frog story as an analogy to the corporate world, obviously no individual or organization wants to end up as a boiled frog, but that is exactly what can and does happen. One strategy to prevent that happening is through systematic monitoring and assessing to identify the directional trend of small incremental changes that cumulatively can have a major and sometimes devastating impact. We need some type of barometer to monitor climate changes in our business and organizational environments, recording what happens so that we detect the patterns. Indeed, as the frog story indicates, that can be the difference between death and survival.

Adapt through learning

Another strategy for any individual to effectively manage change is to consistently acquire new skills and knowledge. With a greater range of skills, knowledge and improved competencies, you are better able to adapt or exploit external changes as they occur in your wider world. You are ready for change. A related advantage of consistently improving and learning is that, by doing so, you will expand your frame of reference, which broadens the scope of potential opportunities available to advance yourself and those around you.

The same strategy also applies to teams and organizations. By consistently improving core competencies and learning new ways to do things, a team or organization can help ensure its survival and prosperity by maintaining competitive advantage against existing and potential competitors. It is up to the individuals within teams and organizations to learn and develop those competencies, but as a leader take the initiative to recognize and facilitate the opportunities to do so both for yourself and for others.

Transformational changes

Major transformational changes are hard to miss. They can be unsettling because of their magnitude and their implications. Although transformational changes do not necessarily threaten our way of life or the structure and systems in which we operate, they do call for our prompt attention and prompt response.

Fortunately, transformational changes are usually relatively easy to handle, because to begin with, we become aware of them when they happen or sometimes we see them approaching. Since we are aware of them as they occur, we tend to quickly react to them. Generally, people and organizations do not need to be convinced of the need to respond to major change, as they might need to be for less obvious incremental change. A reason for this is that people often respond according to the magnitude of change. The greater the change, the more likely the response will be of similar magnitude to match or exceed that of the change. That is why the first frog attempted to leap out of the boiling water, whereas the second frog did not even realize the water temperature was increasing.

Expressed another way, no organization or individual can afford to be fine tuning and playing at the edges with incremental changes when there is transformational change happening. Look at the change, see what is really happening, and respond accordingly.

Reinvention

If necessity is the mother of invention, then radical change is the mother of reinvention. People, businesses and organizations frequently reinvent themselves. Reinvention goes beyond transformation. Reinvention is analogous to being born again, but leaping straight to adulthood without going through childhood.

Reinvention is the most difficult of all changes due to its immediate and frequently devastating impacts upon us, upon our way of life and upon our organizations. We do well to react swiftly. Reinvention results in a completely new way of thinking, doing and being. Under such circumstances we need to reconsider our aspirations, our actions and our sense of achievement.

We are not used to reinvention or radical change because it rarely happens in the wider, external world. Such change is perhaps a once in a generation or once in a lifetime event. When we experience change of such magnitude we often do not know how to handle it because it is so intense and often devastating in its impact. We are not comfortable with the new situation because we do not know what the new rules are, we do not know what the new system will be that replaces the old system, and we have no idea how to manage what we do not know. We may simply be unaware of what is really going on. It is little wonder then that we feel very uncomfortable. Our personal survival is threatened when the world around us changes to the extent that it reinvents itself and is not at all the world we used to know.

Although any particular event may be unforeseeable, it can be beneficial to consider contingencies for such changes. One approach is to conduct 'what if' scenarios based upon 'what if the world as we know it, changed?' How would you and your organization reinvent yourselves? What would you actually do? If you could not provide the same products or services, what other products or services could you provide? What structure and systems would you need? The benefit of going through such an exercise is that it can produce a completely better way of doing something, or identify totally new avenues of business.

On a personal level, to meet such enormous challenges could require creating a 'new you': that is, you may need to reinvent yourself. To reinvent yourself could include changing your career into a completely new field; relocating to a new area or a new country where there are better opportunities for you; or taking a radically different approach to what you are currently doing. Absolute Leaders realize that by developing flexibility, adaptability, foresight and taking the necessary actions, they can reinvent themselves and their organizations to suit almost any situation.

Responding to external change

There are four fundamental responses to external change, being: (i) do nothing; (ii) leave; (iii) change the situation; and, (iv) adapt yourself.

The first option, to do nothing, is the easiest choice for most people because they 'respond by not responding'. By doing nothing they are really denying and resisting change, usually hoping that it will go away. They continue without adapting themselves to the new situation or environment. Later, when they realize how little progress they have made, they wonder why they do not achieve the same or better results as they did before. It is because of their unwillingness to adapt that they ignore the fact that they continue doing exactly what they did previously. Either they cannot understand it, or they deny it. They often look for the answers in the wrong places, by blaming others or blaming the changed circumstances, but there is no net value gained whatsoever from blaming. So just hoping for better results is unrealistic because in all likelihood the results will be worse, since hopes and expectations are not backed by different actions necessary to address different situations.

The second option is to leave or opt out. This is a change in itself because the people leaving end up facing new environments. The risk is they do not like the new environments they choose, they fail to fit in with them, so they sooner or later leave each one until they eventually find someplace else where they think it suits them better.

The third and fourth options are respectively, to change the situation or to adapt yourself, the latter of these providing the greatest possibilities, not just for survival but also for prosperity.

Change the situation

As an individual, you cannot change the macro, bigger picture of external circumstances beyond the control of you and your organization, but you may be able to change your own individual situation at work, or that of your team or organization.

For example, you could be working in an organization that is very process driven, inhibiting the ability of your organization to respond to a dramatic change in economic or business conditions (such as a market crash). One thing that you might be able to do is come up with a method to fast track decision making in a critical area, thereby facilitating your organization to respond to change quicker than previously. You could accomplish that by looking for a way to circumvent the formal management structure without threatening it; pilot schemes and special projects quickly come to mind as potential strategies. Alternatively, you may come up with ways to modify products or services to better suit them to the changed demands of your customers. Yet another option is to create innovative new products and services for the new business environment, in a sense creating a new market. The difference between standing still and changing could be critical to the survival of your organization, and to you.

Adapt yourself

The keys to adapting yourself include committing to personal change, replacing whatever has passed its use by date, responding quickly, and being flexible.

Commit to personal change

Positively changing and adapting yourself is a lot easier to do than trying to get the rest of the world to change and adapt to you!

The beauty of changing yourself is that you become the dominant influence of the change process and of the outcomes. You can be in charge and be the 'driver' responsible for taking the initiatives to change yourself personally and professionally at any time. It is up to you.

There is much about you that you can change, including how you think and what you do. In addition, you can change your emotional attachment to whatever no longer serves your aspirations. To bring about whatever changes you desire, be prepared to commit and persevere with the necessary actions. You may not be able to change your personality, but changing behavior is definitely possible. People do that everyday, with behavioral coaching being one of the methods used. Changing behavior requires commitment, but learning to conduct yourself more successfully in a greater variety of situations and with different people is incredibly rewarding and satisfying. Ultimately, the most viable option you have available is to change and adapt yourself.

Replace what has expired

All of us have things that come to the end of their expiry or use by dates. Their time is up. Some of our thought patterns and habits are welcome to begin with but eventually they can serve no useful purpose. Indeed, they become a significant hindrance to our progress. We need to replace or upgrade them with patterns and habits that are more helpful to us.

Consider whatever does not serve you as well as it did before. Now is the time to change or replace it. Amongst other possibilities, you may benefit by learning new skills such as improving your existing competencies in areas such as communication; leveraging your networks; seeking new ideas; using your support teams; managing stress better; overcoming limiting beliefs and fears; tracking your progress; taking greater responsibility; improving your interpersonal skills; improving your negotiating skills; and, empowering others.

Respond quickly

One way Absolute Leaders differentiate themselves is by the speed with which they anticipate and adapt to changes in their business or organizational environment. It can take you out of a comfort zone, but do not let that stop you from making necessary changes. Changing yourself is the most positive and powerful way of handling change, and it is often the quickest path you can take. It improves your results, your productivity, your motivation, your self-confidence, your enjoyment, and your sense of accomplishment.

When transformational change or reinvention happens in your environment, respond quickly. Do not assume things will eventually return to where they were because they will never return. The world moves forward, not backward. The quicker you respond the better off you will be.

If you do not respond quick enough to change, you will be left behind, not only by the world around you, but also by other people. Thinking you can continue as before is fraught with risk, it is self-defeating. You will be left standing still when all around you are moving. It is like being in the driver's seat of a car waiting at the traffic lights on a multi-lane road. The red traffic light is on, you are stationary with the transmission in neutral, the handbrake is on, and your foot is on the brake pedal. When the light changes to green you need to shift into forward gear, remove the handbrake, take your foot off the brake and press on the accelerator. Why? It is because your environment has changed! The traffic light has gone from red to green, signaling for you and every other driver to move. Other drivers accelerate and take off, so if you do not do the same you are left behind. Push hard on the accelerator!

Be flexible

History teaches that many civilizations and societies come to their end during their peak. Frequently the reason is that the systems and structures that initially stabilize and endure them eventually become so inflexible that they cannot adapt to change. Irrespective of who challenges them, they also believe that their established structures and systems will help them endure and reign supreme, no matter the potential threat. They believe in the glory of their history rather than the reality of their present circumstances and the possibility for a different, although better future. To some individuals, this description of inflexibility may well sound like their own organization, or perhaps other individuals whom they know.

Be flexible. When you need to, be prepared to change your strategy, your structure and your 'modus operandi', as conditions and situations demand. Review the changes you plan to make, think them through, but ultimately do what you must. The same structures, strategies and systems, are unlikely to all work effectively in all situations at all times. As you progress through your career and through the development stages of your business or organization, adapt yourself and your actions as necessary.

Help others adapt

One key role of Absolute Leaders is helping other people adapt themselves to change. The natural tendency of most people is to remain in their comfort zone, thereby resisting change. To personally change or adapt, they often need a compelling reason that must make both rational sense as well as appeal to them at an emotional level. A rational, logical reason will provide the justification whereas appealing to emotion will give the necessary buy-in at a personal level to make the decision to change or adapt.

Clarifying the needed changes, in the context of team and organizational vision or aspirations, is one approach. Context is better understood when people see the bigger picture. As part of the clarification process, the bigger picture context should ideally be supported with a business case and an implementation strategy for the required changes. The aim is to highlight how an individual's teams, business unit or organization can survive, and thrive, through adaptation and change, and to identify the necessary steps to bring that about.

Effective adaptation involves letting go of, or losing, something that can be replaced with something more beneficial. Ascertain what is being lost and quantify its lower value relative to the value of making changes. Helping others to understand at a personal level and situational context the value of what they are relinquishing usually helps them better deal with and adapt to change.

Since individuals are more likely to engage emotionally if they are actively involved in the change process, the earlier they engage in the change or adaptation process, the better for everyone. Soliciting suggestions from those affected by the changes and how to implement them is a vital step in any change strategy. Through that process they can personally drive change from where they are in a business or organization, so that change happens from the 'bottom-up', or 'sideways-across', rather than being seen as something that is only imposed top-down from senior management.

COMPETENCY 3

Energize for growth

"Fortune favors the brave."

Roman proverb

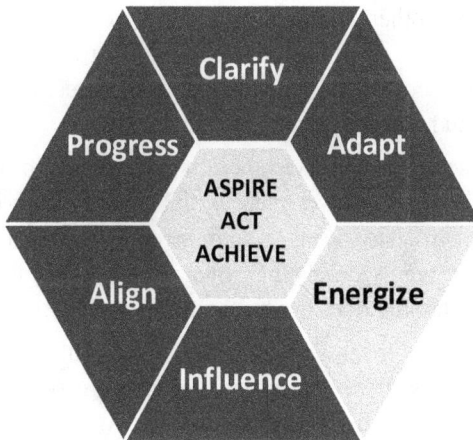

Energy gives life

Energy gives life and feeds growth, so it is essential to harness your positive energy for your own wellbeing. Whether you are charismatic or quiet, radiating positive energy to other people will help draw them towards you.

The importance of positive energy

Most people can relate to having entered a room and immediately felt there was a positive or negative energy present. It is the atmosphere in the room. Often people experience a very strong positive energy when they are in a particular location (even in a different spot within the same room), or in the presence of particular people. Why?

Firstly, it happens because everything and everyone has energy. Secondly, both positive or negative energy is radiated or transmitted to other places and people. As individuals, we sense the 'vibes' of that radiated energy. Most significantly for leadership, we radiate or vibrate our own energy to other people and they sense our vibes. At work, we bring our energy into the work environment and affect the working climate or atmosphere.

It follows that if we have negative energy, we will send negative vibrations to others and create a negative atmosphere. Similarly, if we have positive energy then others will feel positive vibes when they are around us, or communicating with us. Energy is often experienced as a vibration even before we meet someone. It is important to radiate positive energy to other people, even if you have not previously met them.

Positive energy has a power about it that appeals to other people and usually makes them want to connect with, tap into, and be a part of it. Negative energy can also appeal to some people, but most people want to avoid it because it merely drains their own positive energy; for that reason, complaining and blaming does not have a positive impact upon people.

At an individual level, you are solely responsible to create, build and maintain your own positive energy level. There are two ways to do that. The first is to rid yourself of negative energy, for the simple reason that holding onto negative energy makes it very difficult, if not impossible, to replace it with positive energy. You cannot feel both positive and negative about the same thing at the same time. The second thing to do is to immerse yourself in positive thoughts, behaviors and emotions, that increase your levels of positive energy. You will be better for it, and other people will tap into and respond to your positive vibes. In that way you help create a positive atmosphere in your workplace and also in your private life.

Positive energy is strongly associated with optimism and positive expectations. A person who is highly optimistic will tend to display high levels of positive energy. By contrast, a person who has substantially negative energy is more than likely to be oriented or 'anchored' in an unsatisfying past or be pessimistic about the future.

Three types of human energy

Human energy can be considered as consisting of, (i) Mental or mind, (ii) Physical or body, and (iii) Emotional or spiritual. All three types of energy are interconnected and substantially affect each other.

Emotional energy, especially the energy of negative emotions such as fear, is difficult for many people to handle, but it can be managed and conquered. From an Absolute Leadership perspective, operating in a state of fear, such as the fear of survival, makes it difficult to utilize positive emotions to fulfill one's true potential, even though there is much to be gained from leveraging positive emotions such as hope and passion. The stronger your positive energy, both mentally and physically, the more likely you are to experience positive rather than negative emotions thereby increasing your levels of positive emotional energy.

Mental thoughts and physical actions also require effort to manage well and develop. If you develop positive thoughts you are much more likely to subsequently take the positive actions essential to build healthy habits, thereby increasing your positive physical energy. To take the example of motivation, the mental process of thinking about why you do something so you understand your motivation can make it easier to perform the required actions in a positive manner using positive energy.

Utilizing positive human energy is a critical competency of Absolute Leadership. It takes large amounts of positive energy to lead others, and since energy is expressed and reflected through your thoughts, actions and emotions, the positive energy that you give or vibrate to other people can attract or repel potential followers and supporters.

Charismatic and 'quiet' energy

Most of us know, or have met, people that are charismatic. You may be a charismatic person. Charismatic people seem to display higher levels of energy compared to other 'quieter' people. Quieter people often appear less energetic, and so many people believe that 'quiet' people do not have the requisite energy level to accomplish as much as charismatic people. It is a myth. Quieter people often channel their energy in different ways than charismatic people. The fact is that there are many 'quiet achievers', the numbers of which more than likely exceed the number of charismatic achievers.

Enjoy the passion

If you are not passionate an activity, you are more likely to simply go through the motions of doing it without obtaining a true sense of enjoyment. With passion you will enjoy what you do. By enjoying what you do, you will increase your passion.

Feel the passion

Can we really be passionate about what we do for a career or business? Is it possible to love what we do? Can someone be passionate about going to work each day? Can someone be passionate about attending a meeting at work or preparing a report? The answer to all these questions and others like them is an emphatic 'Yes!' and for Absolute Leaders it is an everyday reality. It is impossible to inspire passion in others if you are not passionate about what you do.

Passion is a very powerful, positive emotion that helps you strive towards your aspirations. When you walk into your workplace each morning, you will perform at a higher level if you are passionate about what you do. You do not necessarily have to love every aspect of your job, but being passionate about it encourages you to take appropriate actions required for higher level performance and personal satisfaction.

To create passion in what you do everyday, link your daily activities and actions to your long-term aspirations and career goals. Make the connection very clear and as direct as you can, so that when you are working you are not simply doing a job, but instead you are actually applying yourself and your passion to your higher goals and aims.

Put your heart and soul into what you do. Become passionate about it, really passionate. Take care and pride in what you do. Look at what you do as your life's calling, imagine it as your life's vocation. Ensure that it connects with you at a mental, physical and emotional level.

Enjoy what you do

People who enjoy what they do, naturally perform better. They take what they do very seriously, yet they retain a sense of humor and enjoyment. Enjoyment in this context is the satisfaction that comes from working to the best of your ability, from achieving what you set out to do, from overcoming obstacles, and from the value and benefits that you, your organization and others, derive as a direct result of your efforts and accomplishments. Irrespective of what you do, one way to increase your performance and satisfaction is to enjoy it more.

Consider what you enjoy about your career and business. Take a moment to make your own list. Some suggestions are made below, but do not confine yourself to them, as there are many other ways that you may derive enjoyment from your role. The things you enjoy about your work may include: making a positive impact in the lives of others; belonging to an elite group of leaders; independence; the thrill of making deals; the interaction with people; the results; financial reward and compensation; working in different locations including other countries; recognition by your colleagues, family and community; practicing your influencing and persuading skills; and, the personal satisfaction of meeting challenges.

Turn new actions into new habits

The first step to developing new, helpful habits is removing established negative habits that are detrimental to your aspirations. The second step is consciously engaging in new actions or behaviors so that they become habits. This can be painful to begin with, but if you persist, your new behaviors eventually become very pleasurable as you become the manifestation of your new habits.

Remove undesirable habits

As Aristotle said, "We are what we repeatedly do". Our habits are automatic responses that have worked for us, or at least we think they have. They are such an integral part of who we are that they seem to serve our purposes, even if at times we are not aware of, or clear about, our purposes. Not surprisingly, when we lack clarity about our long-terms aims, less desirable habits tend to take over. We may find ourselves doing things through habit when we know that alternative behaviors would be far more beneficial for us and for those around us.

The good news about habits is that we can unwire the connections in our brains to eliminate undesirable habits. We can remove habits that we no longer desire, that no longer serve our purposes and aspirations. There is no need to keep repeating habits that are detrimental to us. Habits that do not serve what we aspire to can be stopped and eliminated from our automatic response mechanism. The trap with undesirable habits is that we keep running them much like an autopilot programmed for a destination we do not really want to visit. The solution to undoing automatic habits, is to take over the controls and seize personal command to fly to the destination of your choice.

Think about your existing habits and identify those that no longer serve your best interests. They are the habits that impede your aspirational success and goals. Of those, select just one and try to catch yourself next time you slip into that habit. Stop and ask yourself why you are doing something that has no value to you. It makes no sense to keep repeating it. Repeat this exercise of catching yourself each time you repeat the habit, so that you begin to interrupt the automatic wiring or connections in your brain that usually lead you to act that way. By consistently breaking the repetitive, automatic response mechanism in your brain, you can eventually eliminate the undesirable habit. By repeatedly interrupting your existing automatic response, you are more likely to bring about an alternative course of new action and develop a new automatic response.

Use your brain's plasticity to form new habits

We can rewire our brains to form and develop new habits that allow us to function in ways that will help us achieve our full potential. Neuroscience has taught us that the adult brain is capable of building new neural connections because it has a high level of plasticity. Plasticity does not mean that the brain is plastic, but rather that the brain can be molded in a functional sense according to how it is used. The parts of your brain that you use more often will develop more than the parts of your brain that you do not use or use less often. The brain does this by forming stronger connections in the brain areas that are used more frequently. In order to have a new thought, action, or emotion take hold, you need to persevere so that your brain will develop the connections required. It is only by repeatedly attempting to make new neural connections and consistently using new connections to strengthen them, that they will work effectively and in time become an 'automatic' way of functioning.

Removing old habits is a lot easier if we have new habits to replace them; in other words, to stop doing something we need something else new to do that replaces the old. Since habits are wired into the functioning of our brains, we tend to respond to new problems and new situations through our same habitual patterns, whether or not they are suitable for a new problem or situation. Therein lays one of the reasons why we find it difficult to change. It is a lot easier and requires no effort not to change, and many people take this easy escape although it is a far less rewarding and far less satisfying option.

One of the key determinants to forming a new habit is the frequency with which you use the new behavior. The more you use any new behavior, the quicker and stronger the automatic circuitry and connections in your brain develop for a new habit to take hold, thereby becoming an integral part of you. It really does not take very long to acquire a new habit if you make the conscious effort to apply yourself.

To develop a new habit or a new skill also requires vigilant practice. To illustrate, training programs teach people new skills, but the value of training rises dramatically when the learning is used and practiced in the workplace. By putting new learning into practice often enough and by consciously applying new learning, its practice or action becomes 'automatic' and eventually it becomes a new habitual skill that people can do automatically without thinking. By contrast, if what is learnt is not put into practice, most, if not all of it, is soon forgotten.

Move from pain to pleasure

It takes big healthy doses of personal determination and self-discipline to develop a new habit. Repeatedly practicing a new behavior is essential to turn it into a habit. Doing something once or twice or for a short-term, does not create a habit. Repeated practice is a proven means to wire a new behavioral circuit into your brain in order for a new activity to become a new habit.

The natural tendency of most people is to try something once or twice, then, if they find it is difficult, they give up. They expect too much too soon from too little effort. This is all the more so when people do not see immediate results, which is why it is important to have meaningful aspirations and a clear picture or vision of what they want to eventually achieve. To learn something new, for something new to become part of ourselves, requires constant repetition and practice: the more repetition and practice the better. Initially, a new action or behavior is likely to be discomforting, even painful, but, as we persist in using it, the level of pain gradually dissipates as it becomes easier and more pleasurable to do.

A useful analogy is exercise. Let us say for example, that a person wants to improve her health and fitness by jogging. She goes jogging, and the first time out, after just a short distance, her calf muscles begin to ache. They ache because they are not conditioned to jogging. The next day she decides to go jogging and the same thing happens again; her calf muscles ache. However, this time, and perhaps without realizing it, she jogs just a little further than she did the day before. She does this repeatedly most days for several weeks, eventually managing to jog a reasonable distance without experiencing too much pain in her calves. She notices that some days her calves do not ache at all, or no longer ache over the same distance as they did on previous days. What happens is that her muscles form the habit of being able to perform over the distance without problem or pain. She is then able to jog the distance easily. Indeed, she is progressively able to jog a lot further without experiencing pain. The more frequently she goes jogging, the easier and more pleasurable it becomes. Her jogging transforms from aches and pains into pleasure! Eventually her muscles and her body adapt so well to the jogging that it becomes something she does automatically, helping her to achieve her health and fitness goals. As a result, she feels good about herself, transforming jogging into a pleasurable experience.

The same 'pain to pleasure' principle applies to forming new habits for virtually anything. The starting point is to have a goal. The next step is to take action and experience the pain or discomfort of doing something that you are not used to. By doing it repeatedly, the initial pain will disappear and the activity, eventually, becomes pleasurable.

Reprogram yourself

Various techniques are available for you to reprogram yourself. Included amongst them are the ability to visualize yourself being successful; learning to think, act and feel successful and using affirmations.

Visualize yourself being successful

It is a lot easier to be successful and accomplish anything if you can first visualize yourself being the person you seek to be and living the life you wish to live. This is because you get to experience the success of the particular behaviors you focus on in your mind before they happen in reality, before you actually perform them in real time. It can be said that you get to experience everything at least twice, firstly in your mind then secondly in the physical world.

Visualization is a powerful tool and you can apply visualization techniques for any specific behaviors or actions. Absolute Leaders visualize themselves as being successful (the destination) and as conducting themselves successfully (the journey). They visualize much of what they do, and visualize often enough that it becomes automatic for them. Visualizing becomes a habit. At first, visualizing is a very deliberate conscious activity, but over time it can become an automatic part of how you function. By practicing and repeating visualizations, you can rewire the circuitry of your brain to create mental images and visions that you want to experience in the real world. With sufficient practice, you can learn to literally switch on your visualizations at any moment you wish.

The great power of visualization is its ability to influence the subconscious mind. The reason it works is because the mind either does not distinguish, or finds it hard to distinguish, between what is imagined as a visualization and what really occurs in the physical world. In short, your mind cannot tell the difference between what you imagine and reality. Therefore, if you visualize an event such as a negotiation, when you come to actually negotiate, it is easier to do because your mind has already 'experienced' the negotiation event. That same visualization technique can be applied to virtually any event or activity.

Think, act and feel successful

Absolute Leaders conduct themselves as professionally successful at all times. Doing so means to think, act and feel successful at any moment. Think as if you are already as successful as you intend to be, and as far as you can do the very things that you imagine you will do when you achieve your ultimate aspirations. In that way, you can experience for yourself now and at any moment you choose, the feeling of living and leading the life that you imagine, both in your private life and in your career.

It does not matter whether you think you have already achieved success or not (since in any case that is your perception). Achieving your aspirations comes about by conducting yourself as the person you aspire to be. You cannot afford to wait for some particular event or future time to occur before you begin to act appropriately. Immerse yourself now into thinking, doing, living and experiencing, whatever it is that you seek to achieve.

Use positive affirmations

Positive affirmations are brief statements you write in your own words to repeat to yourself frequently. They are your personal mantras, in some respects being a form of prayer. Through repetition, they influence and condition your subconscious mind. Your subconscious mind, in turn, influences your thoughts, emotions and behavior. Therefore, if you want to think, feel and act positively, the pre-step is to embed into your subconscious mind positive ideas about yourself that you want to become a part of you. You can do that by using positive affirmations.

To be effective, your affirmations must have meaning. The ideal way to give them meaning is for your affirmations to express something you want to be or achieve, or to express qualities that you want to develop or acquire, such as the six competencies of Absolute Leadership. Your affirmations must be specific, since it is through specificity and focus combined with repetition, that your affirmations produce the intended result. For greater effectiveness, state your affirmations in the present tense, using "I am…" rather than "I will…" For example, stating "I am clear about my purpose" is far more effective than "I will clarify my purpose". Repeat your affirmations regularly, preferably at least once everyday.

To err is human

People make mistakes. The aim is not to repeat them. Mistakes can be minimized by understanding that the world is not necessarily perfect as we want it to be, and by being able to recognize and ask when we need help.

The imperfect nature of perfection

Reflecting upon a place he had visited long ago, a physicist once related a story to me concluding with the observation that, "There is no such thing as the edge of the world but from some places you can almost see it!" The same applies to perfection. Maybe perfection is out there somewhere, and if we could somehow get close enough we could almost see it, but no matter what we do, it seems to be elusive.

The notion of what is 'perfect' is opinion based. Therefore, even when something can be measured for perfection, since the technical definition is subjective, it follows that the definition is subject to imperfection itself. In other words, the idea of perfection is itself imperfect!

Just look at the world around you and consider how well it fits with any notions you have of perfection. Imperfections seem to abound. That being said does not imply that imperfection should be a goal, on the contrary it is to recognize its prevalence and learn to manage and live with it up to a point. It does not negate the need to set standards and targets to achieve and improve beyond those already accomplished. Perfection is most likely not the target, but making improvements and progress is a much more realistic and achievable option.

Seeking perfection can easily lead to obsession, frustration and extreme control. Such behaviors run counter-productive to that which is really important. People do not want to be controlled, but they do want matters to be under control, because reasonably predictable matters are easier to deal with for most people.

Associated with imperfection or perfection (depending upon your viewpoint), is the notion that we should be able to control most things, if not everything we do, as well as control the people and the environment around us. As a society, as organizations and as individuals, we can easily become control obsessed, promulgating a belief that through control we can bring about perfection. However, seeking perfection usually diminishes control, whereas tolerating acceptable degrees of imperfection brings matters and situations under control.

Another way to consider perfection is that perhaps everything is already perfect as it is or many things are as perfect as they can be, but what creates imperfection are our attempts to control.

Learn from mistakes

Mistakes provide the opportunity to evolve, change and grow. Although the least painful mistakes from which to learn are the mistakes of others, it seems that most people insist upon experiencing their own mistakes!

The first step in learning from any of our mistakes is to recognize and admit them to ourselves. Then assess what went wrong. What did we do that was OK? What could we have done differently? What should we have known before we acted? Were the wrong people involved? How can we involve the right people next time? Were we too impulsive or too slow off the mark? Did we listen to our intuition? Was the timing wrong? How may it be possible to obtain a better outcome when we are next in a similar situation?

Absolute Leaders learn once from their mistakes and do not repeat them. Do something different the next time a similar situation occurs and demonstrate your learning to yourself and others. If what you do differently next time also turns out to be inappropriate, then learn from that and adapt by doing something different yet again the next time, until eventually the right action becomes apparent. Making a mistake the first time is often not avoidable, but repeating it always is.

Ask for help

When you need help, ask! Asking for help frees you. It takes the pressure off. It liberates you. A great thing about asking for help is the willingness of other people to give you help. They support you because they want to see you reap the benefits of their advice and help. In that way they become a stakeholder in your achievements, and they may also experience their own sense of liberation and satisfaction by being able to help you. People will help you if you ask. So ask!

Don't let your ego get in your way

Asking for help can be daunting for some people for a variety of reasons. They may perceive it as an admission that they are out of their depth; or that what they are doing is too hard or too difficult for them; or that they cannot cope; or that they do not have the ability to solve their own problems or someone else's issues; or that in some shape or form they are somehow inadequate; or that they are not as all knowing and masterful as they would like to be. All of that can be hard to cope with, placing enormous stress on people when they project an image of not needing help, but in fact they would really welcome it.

Ego gets in their way!

People often associate asking for help with negative self-worth. Yet the reality is that we increase our self-worth when we ask for help, because it allows us to resolve the matters for which we need help. Doing so allows us to learn the lesson and move forward. We grow personally and professionally as a result of being helped.

Bypass the blame game

Some people take on blame for matters for which they are not personally responsible at all, or they take on a degree of blame for something far more proportional to their actual involvement. In some cases, people take on blame just because they happen to be present at the time although they had nothing to do with the 'blame' event. Inappropriately apportioned blame diminishes the energy and motivation of the people taking on the blame. That in turn reduces their self-belief thereby affecting their performance in their role. In some cases, negative effects can persist throughout their entire career or lifetime.

The moment someone assigns personal blame to someone else, he effectively acknowledges that he does not want to personally address the underlying issue. Interestingly enough, people that blame others for their own shortcomings do not enhance their own self-worth, despite any initial feelings that they have got away with something. The reason they blame someone else is because it is the easy option. Cowardice is much easier than courage, but it is never the better option.

Whether others accept their responsibilities or not is up to them, just as long as you accept yours. Absolute Leaders understand and assist people to accept their responsibilities, but they do not personally take on the unnecessary blame to become a scapegoat for the shortcomings of others.

Move beyond personal inhibitors

Major distractions in our lives inhibit us from moving forward. Fear, including the fear of success, is also a major obstacle for many people.

Resolve distractions promptly

If you have any major distractions in your personal life, they will affect your ability to focus at work and therefore affect your professional performance. The biggest distractions in life are usually those associated with the loss of a partner, divorce and separation, but even something like moving house just down the street or even within the same apartment building, can prove very distracting and work performance suffers accordingly.

Deal with and manage distractions promptly and effectively if you are to focus upon what you do professionally. You cannot be in two places at the same time, whether that is in your mind or physically. Since you can only focus upon one thing at a time, if any type of personal life distraction preoccupies your mind or time, you cannot effectively concentrate upon your work and you will therefore underperform. Likewise, if you have any major distractions at work, they can affect your private life with family and relationships.

If you have a major distraction, try to take some time out to deal with it, and seek professional help to resolve it. Do not bring personal issues to work to talk about them at length with your colleagues or associates. It might make you feel good for a while, but it will ultimately serve you no long-term benefit. Most people have enough of their own personal or professional 'distractions' to contend with, so they do not really want to hear about somebody else's. They might well be sympathetic with you, but no amount of sympathy from anyone can ever help you, and the workplace should never be the arena of choice to resolve personal problems.

The fear of success

Fear is an emotion that is related not only to failing, but also to success. The fear of success is in many ways a fear of failure. It seems ironic that some individuals say they fear success partly because of the unknown impacts that it may have upon their lives. To illustrate, a consequence of success for some individuals might be that they are required to relocate to a new city or country, thereby uprooting them and their family from their established community and support networks. Despite the opportunity, they may not want to run the risk of accepting the responsibility if life does not work out in the new location. Hence, what they really fear is not success but failure, since they fear they will not adapt to their new situation.

Another similar fear experienced by individuals is that success might affect their friendships, in that their long time friends might not like them anymore due to their greater success. The real issue is the individuals' own fear of not remaining authentic to themselves as circumstances change throughout their career advancement. By working through their fears and the possible consequences, and by vividly imagining the worst possible outcomes, individuals can put into perspective and resolve any such fears that potentially inhibit them from being successful.

High physical energy is vital

High physical energy is critically dependent upon both what you eat and regular exercise. Poor diet and a lack of exercise will undermine your physical, mental and emotional wellbeing.

Eat a healthy diet

Good health and vitality is often an undervalued part of success and achievement. Physically healthy people are less prone to stress, they deal with life better, they tend to have higher self-esteem, and they function and perform in a better way. Absolute Leaders appreciate that through the benefits of good health they are more likely to achieve their goals and aspirations.

A healthy diet is fundamental to good health. It helps people attain better health, especially when they combine it with exercise and other energy enhancing activities.

The three basic aspects to a healthy diet are variety, balance, and moderation. Variety is the spice of life and of healthy eating. A diet with good variety is one that provides all the nutrients that you need through a wide range of different food groups, such as fruit, vegetables, meats, dairy products and cereals. It is also beneficial to have variety within any food group, so for example, eating a mix of different vegetables is healthier than eating just one or two types of vegetables. As the human body needs all four major food components, namely fats, proteins, carbohydrates and water, a balanced diet will include adequate amounts of all four food types plus other essential vitamins and nutrients. Eating in moderation means not eating too much of anything or of any major food type, especially over a sustained period.

Natural foods are far better than processed

Natural foods that can be eaten raw, or with minimal cooking, are far healthier than processed foods. It is greatly beneficial to eat plenty of fruits and vegetables, preferably two serves of fruit and three serves of vegetables per day. These are a good source of nutrients and vitamins. With fresh fruits and vegetables, eat them relatively soon after you buy them, as the longer you leave them before eating the less nutritional value they provide. Vegetables that are richest in nutrients are usually deep yellow or dark green in color. Avoid over cooking vegetables because that reduces their nutrient value. Many vegetables can be eaten raw or just lightly steamed. The less that fruit and vegetables are cooked, the more energy and nutrient value they generally provide. Fruits and vegetables that can be eaten raw provide the highest level of nutrients and energy, but a few, such as tomatoes, are more beneficial when cooked.

If you find it difficult to buy fresh vegetables, then frozen vegetables are an excellent substitute, although seldom as far as taste is concerned. In regards to nutrient levels, most frozen vegetables retain much of their original nutrient value. Do not excessively cook frozen vegetables, as all they usually need is defrosting and reheating since they have been cooked just prior to freezing. Canned vegetables are an inferior substitute for either fresh or frozen vegetables. If using canned vegetables, always rinse them thoroughly to reduce the added preservatives. Dry beans or dry vegetables soaked in water before cooking are a better nutritional alternative to the canned alternatives.

Either eliminate eating highly processed foods, or reduce your intake as much as possible. The more processed any food is, generally the harder it is to digest. Most 'white' foods such as white bread are more processed and less beneficial for you than their 'brown' equivalents. Brown breads are healthier than white breads (wholemeal breads being healthier than grain breads). Brown or raw sugar is healthier than white sugar. Brown rice is healthier than white rice, although it takes much longer to cook.

Processed foods such as cured meats (for example, ham and salami) are difficult to digest, smoked meats being especially so. Avoid them, or if you cannot resist eating them, do so only occasionally and in moderate quantities. The same applies to smoked fish such as smoked salmon.

Nuts are a good source of healthy monounsaturated fats, especially if you want to avoid unhealthy saturated fats found in dairy products and fatty animal meat. Nuts are a good source of proteins and antioxidants, but high in calories so only eat small quantities.

The way food is cooked and prepared affects its nutritional value. Fast foods are usually cooked in unhealthy fatty oils (saturated fats) that are not friendly to cholesterol levels, or to waistlines and backsides. Cooking in olive oil is much healthier than cooking in animal fat or butter, because olive oil contains cholesterol friendly monounsaturated fats, whereas the saturated fats in animal fats and butter (as well as in other dairy products) are not cholesterol friendly. Grilled food is much healthier than fried. Many foods such as fish, chicken and vegetables, are suitable for steaming, which is a particularly healthy way to cook.

Low fat diets, fast foods and obesity

If low fat diets are to work at all, both the total amount of energy intake (measured as kilojoules or kJ) needs to be reduced as well as the amount of fat intake. Reducing weight is about reducing total energy intake, not just simply changing the proportional mix of carbohydrates, proteins and fats. In addition, regular exercise is integral to the success of sustained weight loss.

Since all foods have four major components, fats, proteins, carbohydrates and water, when fat is reduced or eliminated from food, as it is in low fat foods, the fat must be replaced by water, proteins or carbohydrates. Fat removed from foods is usually replaced by carbohydrates, often as sugar. Since the energy yield (kJ) per unit of fat is about two times that of carbohydrates and protein, people often eat a lot more low fat food to obtain the same energy value and therefore they never lose weight. People may, fallaciously, believe that by reducing fat they can eat as much as they like of non-fat or low fat foods without increasing their weight. They are woefully mistaken!

Avoid over eating

Eat an adequate amount but avoid eating overly large meals that provide excessive calories and energy. By regularly eating large meals, you habituate your digestive system to larger food intakes, whereas smaller, adequate meals condition your system to more modest intakes. You clearly need to eat sufficient amounts to satisfy your hunger, but eating so much so that you feel bloated is a clear message for you to decrease your food intake. By overeating you will feel sluggish and reduce, rather than increase, your energy level.

A contributing factor to eating excessively is the number of meals and snacks people eat per day. The Western culture tendency is one main meal per day, plus two smaller meals often with snacks (morning and afternoon tea or coffee breaks) in between, the main meal usually being lunch or dinner. In contrast, some Asian cultures eat several smaller meals each day. As to which practice is best, cultural and workplace practices have major influence.

If you can, make breakfast your main meal, or, at the very least, do not skip breakfast. A substantial breakfast can give you energy for a major part of the day. One of the most effective ways to lose excess weight and keep weight off, is to have breakfast rather than lunch or dinner as your main daily meal. If you eat larger breakfasts, then eat smaller lunches and dinners. Also, avoid excessive nibbling and snacking between meals during the day. It is one thing to have a coffee or tea break, but quite another to be continuously snacking or 'grazing'.

In the corporate environment there is regular pressure to attend breakfasts, lunches and dinners. This increases the importance for executives to be aware of what and how much they eat. Again, eating smaller portions, eating healthier prepared foods such as grilled instead of fried, reducing or eliminating alcohol consumption, drinking water, chewing your food well and eating slowly, are all strategies that can help people minimize excess weight gain yet still enjoy the eating occasion at the same time.

The great purifier

Water is the great purifier so drink adequate amounts. About seventy percent of the human body is composed of water. An adult with a balanced diet generally needs to drink between one to two liters of water per day. Caffeine and alcohol dehydrate your body, so if having a coffee or a glass of wine, have a glass of water as well at the same time. The water will also rinse your teeth and reduce staining of your tooth enamel.

Drinking water helps you better digest and flush your digestive system. It helps keep your blood healthier and improves your blood flow. It is good for your skin. It helps wash away toxins in your system. Water helps all functions of your body to function properly. Your body and mind will thank you for drinking it!

Energize through physical fitness

Key elements of physical fitness include regular exercise, good posture and adequate sleep. These should be incorporated into your daily routines.

Exercise regularly

Physical fitness generates energy, reduces stress, and enhances mental alertness. You can do more and achieve more in every part of your life if you are physically fit. That is not to say that fitness is a guarantee for achievement, but it is an important element of Absolute Leadership. You can only put energy into your work by drawing upon your own energy resources. Energy comes from within you but you have to generate it, so use physical exercise to build and maintain your physical energy, as well as your mental and emotional energy levels.

If you are not fit, becoming fit does not happen overnight. It requires discipline and commitment to integrate exercise into your daily and weekly routines. Unfortunately, much of the promotion associated with fitness promises instant results, in a similar fashion to how lotteries promote the major prize to lure people into believing in instant riches without effort, or diets lure people into believing they can become instantly thin. Sustainable fitness requires a long-term approach and it usually takes at least several months or longer for your muscles to transform into sustained fitness mode.

Age is not a barrier to improving fitness, although for some it is an excuse. Many sports programs and activities are available that cover all age ranges. You do not have to be a teenager or rank in the 'Top 100' to play and enjoy sport! People that start an exercise and fitness regime even in their older years often achieve levels of fitness similar to those of people who have been already exercising for many years. The key is to be consistent, making exercise a part of your regular routines.

To become fit and maintain fitness, joining a gym is one option, whilst some other alternatives are walking, jogging, cycling, swimming and team sports. If there is a sport you really enjoyed playing when you were younger, take it up again. Whenever you can and it is practical to do so, walk or bike ride instead of catching a bus, and climb the stairs instead of taking a lift or escalator if it is just one or two floors. Brisk walking is one of the easiest, most natural and beneficial exercises of all that you can do almost anywhere and it uses many of the body's muscles. The human body was designed as a walking machine.

Walking and bike riding are examples of aerobic exercises. Ideally, aerobic exercises should be done in sessions lasting between thirty to sixty minutes at least three days per week, or they can be done everyday if desired. Stretching and flexibility exercises only require about ten to fifteen minutes to do, and like aerobics, preferably done at least three days per week. Strength building exercises that include weights and resistance training are preferably done for up to thirty minutes per session, two or three times per week, but not every day.

Fitness creates energy that helps you manage stress, plus it increases your self-esteem and self-confidence. It improves mental alertness including the ability to make quicker and better decisions. It is also highly beneficial for your emotional well-being. People also generally perceive fit people as being diligent and successful.

Good posture is vital

Maintaining good posture helps you maintain your health, energy and vitality. Bad posture does the opposite and unnecessarily burns more energy than good posture. It takes conscious effort to maintain good posture until it becomes a habit.

Many individuals spend an inordinate amount of time sitting, either at a desk, in a car, train or aeroplane. Amongst the many problems that can result from sitting for extended periods is a tendency to hunch or roll the shoulders, which can unwittingly lead to curvature of the spine. Sitting also weakens the abdominal muscles because, when we sit, we do not exercise them. This often results in the common ailment of lower back pain. Some relatively simple stretch exercises can counter that, such as sit-ups or arching one's body backwards. Building the strength of abdominal muscles also helps reduce lower back pain, because they act as a supportive belt for the lower back.

Good posture makes you feel more confident and it helps inspire other people to have confidence in you. For better sitting posture, keep your feet flat on the ground, your back straight and your neck straight. Besides sitting, posture is important when you stand and when you walk. Physical exercise is vital to improving posture. Good posture is also linked to positive perceptions of success and the ability to influence other people.

Sleep

Having adequate sleep helps us function more effectively when we are awake. If we have enough sleep, we feel alert and function better physically, mentally and emotionally when we are awake. Too much sleep can make us feel sluggish, even tired, whereas too little sleep can make us feel edgy and reactive. The amount of sleep that adults require is usually between seven to eight hours per night, but normally no less than five hours and no more than ten.

People who do not get enough sleep at night will tend to doze off or have micro sleeps during the day to compensate. It is usually obvious when someone dozes off for while, but micro sleeps that last for just a second or several seconds are much harder to detect. Micro sleeps come without warning, creating lapses of attention that impair performance, increasing the propensity to make mistakes, and increasing the risk of poor decisions.

Re-energize at lunchtime

Re-energizing at lunchtime helps you recharge your energy level for the remainder of the day. It helps prevent burnout and is a good way to relieve stress build-up thereby helping you to accomplish more. Two proven ways to re-energize at lunchtime are to either take a brief catnap, or do some physical exercise.

It is widely acknowledged that the early afternoon is when people are at their lowest energy level for the day and least alert. By re-energizing yourself at lunchtime you will be more alert and more productive for the remainder of the day. By lunchtime, your energy level drops significantly because you have used much of the energy you obtained from your breakfast and your previous night's sleep. In addition, a large lunch, especially one with plenty of carbohydrates, can have the effect of reducing your energy level and alertness soon afterwards, thereby detrimentally affecting your performance in the afternoon (a good argument for the practice of afternoon siestas in Latin countries being adopted worldwide). A protein rather than carbohydrate lunch will assist your alertness for the afternoon.

One way of reenergizing is to catnap. However, it is important to realize that lunchtime catnaps do not involve having a siesta! To be effective, catnaps should be between ten to twenty minutes maximum. Any longer than that, and you are probably sleeping. To catnap, sit in a chair, feet flat on the ground, back straight and upright, with your hands placed flat on your knees. Close your eyes, breathe deeply, relax and drift into the twilight zone. A variation on catnapping is to go somewhere quiet where, without interruption, you can go into a meditative state of mind for a short while.

An alternative to the lunchtime catnap is physical exercise. This also reinvigorates and reenergizes you for the remainder of the day. It is why you often see people jogging or in gyms at lunchtime; they usually come back to work recharged. It helps maintain your overall fitness, health and energy level. If you exercise at lunchtime you are also more likely to eat a smaller lunch, which helps to reduce or stabilize your weight.

Handle and leverage stress

Stress is one of the biggest issues confronting people in the workplace. Some stress is beneficial, but too much or too little leads to dysfunctional performance. Learn to incorporate stress management techniques into your daily lifestyle.

Manage the stress spectrum

Especially in difficult economic times, highly competitive markets, or periods of major change, individuals are under greater than usual pressure to lead and manage their teams and organizations. Their responsibilities for performance at individual, team, business unit and organizational levels become even more critical, because the very survival of a business or organization, not just its growth, is ever more dependent upon their performance.

One way that Absolute Leaders deal with those pressures is by managing and leveraging stress. Some moderate stress is beneficial to perform better. People operating under moderate stress tend to be more resourceful and creative to meet performance targets, thereby functioning at higher or more optimal levels.

With very high levels of stress, it is not uncommon for people to underperform, or even 'burn out' in extreme cases. With too little or no stress, complacency can creep in also resulting in underperformance. At both ends of the stress spectrum, with either extreme stress or too little stress, people become dysfunctional and their performance suffers accordingly.

Be aware of your stress level and ascertain whether your stress originates externally from your workplace and wider environment, or if it is internal coming from within you. When stress is external there is often a sense of inability to reduce the stress. However, try to do whatever you can to minimize the external stress coming from the situation in which you find yourself. Try to change or influence the situation. Do not personally take on board the stresses or the burdens of the world and of other people, that do not belong to you. By contrast, internal stress indicates that there is something within you to address. It could be work related such as skills competency, or it could be something happening in your personal life. Either way it needs to be resolved.

Change your perspective

One way to manage stress is to take a different perspective to its cause. Look at whatever is causing it through different filters. Change your paradigms to see different perspectives. For example, if a problem is connected to a system, the same system will usually keep producing the same types of problems. Such systematic problems are not of your making, so do not take on the associated stress (unless you created the system!).

In other cases, stress can be related to working with or having to deal with a particular person. If you keep dealing with the same person the same way you will keep having the same issues. The answer is to use a different strategy and tactics with the person. You will find that hard to do if you keep approaching the person from the same perspective. Try to look at what the person is doing from another perspective. Develop an understanding of the other person's motivation, then try to devise different approaches, perhaps by involving the person more (or less), or using the influence of another person such as a mutual stakeholder.

Keep your 'cool'

Everyone has a rational 'cool' brain system and an emotional 'hot' brain system. The emotional hot brain system serves as a survival mechanism for when we are threatened or facing fear, particularly for life or death situations. It has one of two impulsive reactions, being either fight or flight. Both reactions are highly emotional and when triggered they happen without thinking.

By contrast, the rational cool brain system, based in the cortex of the brain, is where we process our thoughts. When we receive an external stimulus, our cool brain system ascertains if it is harmful or safe, threatening or non-threatening. We can then respond with our cool brain in a logical and controlled manner.

When people are overly stressed, the emotional hot brain often tends to take over, so that they react impulsively. The impulsive reactions emanate from negative emotions associated with threat to our personal safety. When that happens people can be inclined to literally 'lose it', since they lose the temporary use of their cool, rational brain. Problems occur if they unnecessarily overreact to a situation over what their cool brain would interpret as a minor matter. The key is to manage your emotions and therefore your behavior, by ensuring that your hot brain system does not emotionally hijack what should be logical cool brain responses. In a nutshell, keep your cool!

Meditate

Meditation provides many benefits, amongst them being to increase your energy level and ability to focus. It is also a way of creating personal 'time out' and managing stress.

Through breathing meditation, for example, your total concentration on breathing helps you relax. Meditation through deep breathing also increases your oxygen uptake, which is vital for proper bodily and brain functioning. In the fast paced business world, the ability to breathe deeply is a skill that can help bring a very quick calmness and focus at almost any time and to any situation. Many people are familiar with a mini breathing meditation whereby they stop and take several slow, deep breaths, focusing upon the inhaling and exhaling of each breath. This mini breathing meditation can instantly de-stress people.

Meditation is simultaneously energizing and calming. Most people perform well when they are calm even though they may work under very stressful situations. Many professionals and business people, whilst not necessarily dealing with human life and death issues, do often work in very high-pressure environments where in order to perform at their best they need to be calm. It is not a matter of being calm before the storm, but rather of being calm during each and every storm.

Meditation can help develop calm beneficial for improved performance. There are numerous other benefits such as the positive impact meditation can have upon your interactions with others. Meditation, like most things worthwhile, takes practice and persistence. It is a form of mind exercise, and like its physical exercise counterpart, it requires time to develop and include into your regular routine.

Many people cite lack of time as an excuse not to meditate or exercise. Again, it comes down to personal aspirations and priorities. If meditation can help you to be more relaxed, focus better, and in turn you function more effectively, it is up to you to decide whether the benefits are worth investing your time. It is a lot easier simply to fill your time with low value activities such as watching television, which might keep you informed or entertained, but add little real value to your personal growth and professional development.

Yoga

Physical yoga is a fitness technique that integrates body, mind and spirit, and can be an effective way to build fitness and help manage stress. It primarily involves improving body alignment and flexibility through holding the body in a variety of postures of differing complexity that require mental concentration and breathing to perform. Practicing the postures helps build physical energy and balance, but to do so requires mental focus, thereby connecting the body and mind in the performance of the postures.

Amongst the benefits of yoga is its effect upon the subconscious. By using the physical postures as a means of focusing upon the elements of balance and alignment, those elements are developed in the subconscious mind. Subsequently, that allows them to be utilized for mental and cognitive functions such as decision making, not just for physical functions.

The same principle extends into personal behavior. For example, learning physical alignment from yoga postures can assist you to better understand and apply the principle of alignment to your actions in your workplace. Once you learn the principle, applying it in different situations is easier to do.

Laugh!

Absolute Leaders have a sense of humor and they laugh.

Humor sets us up and reminds us how gullible we really can be. When waiting for the punch line in a joke, although we already know a punch line is coming we still hang in there waiting for it so we can laugh. When the punch line arrives we can usually share our laughter with others (provided they also get the joke), in that way building our communication and connection with them.

Laughing helps us put matters and people, most importantly ourselves and what we do, into perspective. Everything we do might be important, but perhaps it is being able to laugh at ourselves that is the most important thing we can ever do. Humor is about people. It is created through the things that people do and how they react to different situations and other people. Often humor is created because of the unexpected, in that people might have unexpected reactions to something. At other times humor can arise because people are so predictable.

Laughing is a stress breaker.

It is an emotional release because it connects with our deepest emotions and beliefs. For that reason, sometimes we can laugh so much that we cry! We enjoy humor because for most of the time, we live in a world that can be far too serious for our own good and for our own health. Have you ever noticed that people who take everything too seriously do not seem to laugh much, if at all? Perhaps it is because they do not appreciate that having a sense of humor is a very serious matter!

COMPETENCY 4

Influence for understanding

"People ask you for criticism but they only want praise."

W Somerset Maugham, British novelist, 1874 – 1965

Understand behavioral styles

Understanding behavior is critical to influencing others. Everyone has behavioral styles, which is the way that individuals predominantly conduct themselves in their interactions with others. A three stage strategy to understand the influence of behavioral styles begins, firstly, with identifying your own behavioral style or styles. Secondly, identify the behavioral styles of others. Finally, adapt your personal behavior to different situations and different people.

There are numerous ways to profile behavioral styles. One method of behavioral profiling that is helpful and relatively easy to utilize, is based upon both the level of assertiveness of individuals and whether individuals are oriented to things or to people. On that basis, four behavioral styles emerge, namely, (i) Rulers, (ii) Influencers, (iii) Socializers, and (iv) Analyzers.

As you read the following descriptions of the four behavioral styles, try to identify your own major behavioral type. You may find, as many people frequently do for themselves, that you have a combination of two major styles with your behavior, oscillating from one style to the other depending upon circumstance and situation. It is not uncommon, for example, for people to realize that at home, they predominantly use one style of behavior, but use a different style at work, due to the differences of situation, people and environments between the two.

Rulers

Ruler types like to take charge and control. They want power and they use it. Their power is based upon their role or position; what they know; the deals they are involved in; and, the contacts they have. They aim for positions of authority where they can exercise their power in all its various forms.

Rulers focus almost exclusively upon results and therefore the bottom line or profit is what matters most to them and it is the one critical measure they have for making decisions, which they revel in doing. Once they make a decision, they will do 'whatever it takes', persisting, no matter what the obstacles. This can be a great attribute to accomplishment, but like everything can have a shadow side when they push their assertiveness into the realms of dysfunctional aggression that undoubtedly include various forms of intimidation.

As Rulers like to get things done, they take pride in how busy they are. They like to be busier than anyone else and they prefer to be involved in as many things as possible, which is partly why they do manage to complete a great amount.

Rulers generally do not like working in teams because they are highly self-directed individuals and consider that they do not need someone else to motivate them. In addition, they are comfortable to divide and rule. They would prefer that other team members spend their time actually working or 'doing', instead of 'wasting' their time at meetings. In team meetings, they just want to get down to discussing only the business at hand without small talk. Perhaps not surprisingly they view people largely as an economic resource. When they socialize they do so predominantly to advance their business or career, rather than to derive any personal satisfaction from social interaction.

Ruler types are often great entrepreneurs able to get new ventures off the ground. They are also the individuals most likely to turn around organizations that are in crisis. Their power, ability to make decisions, their clarity of purpose, willingness to confront issues and people, are all elements that attract other people to follow them up to a point. Others are often quite willing to let Rulers take charge, effectively handing over control to them, because even though they may not particularly like the style of Rulers, they feel reassured knowing that someone is 'steering the ship'.

Influencers

Influencers are the masters of obtaining results through others. They naturally work with and through other people. They are the great communicators, spending much of their time in dialogue with others. They like to talk and they know how to talk with just about anyone, but they can lose interest very quickly when it comes to the details.

The perceptions of others are paramount to Influencers because they understand the value of image in successful persuasion. Acceptance and appreciation by others is also important to Influencers since they 'like to be liked', so when they need to be very blunt with someone about an issue they often find that difficult to do. In conflict situations, they usually place significant value upon the relationship, not just the outcomes, approaching negotiations from a win/win perspective. If they place overly high importance on relationships, it can inhibit their decision making effectiveness and ability to achieve outcomes.

People are attracted to Influence type leaders because of their open dialogue and genuine interest in people, which many find personally inspiring and motivating, if not at times a little overwhelming. Their usually excellent communication skills generally appeal to others allowing them to quickly establish trust and attract followers.

Influencers like working in teams because teams provide them with opportunities to express their ideas and opinions in what they see as 'theatre'. They are happy to take the lead role on centre stage, the team environment providing the perfect venue. One of the virtues of Influencers is that they are usually great networkers. They often have an array of contacts and personally know the 'who is who' of their profession or industry. As a result, they are able to mobilize other people as well as bring a broad range of viewpoints to different issues.

Socializers

Socializers are friendly, considerate, traditional, and like interacting one-to-one or with small groups of people with whom they are familiar. They genuinely like other people and tend to build strong personal relationships, although often only with a handful of people, so their social and industry networks are usually not very expansive.

Socializers are calm and patient people that seldom like to openly challenge others for fear of conflict. They are comfortable in knowing what they know, and they do not like to be challenged by the comments of others in their area of expertise. Being comfortable with what they know, Socializers generally view change, innovation and new ideas, as potentially threatening instead of as opportunities. Their conservative nature is reflected in their aversion to risk. For example, if asked to attend a brainstorming session they will often privately brainstorm in isolation ahead of the meeting so that they come prepared and knowing they can contribute. The advantage of advance preparation is that Socializers make a conscious, although not especially spontaneous contribution to new ideas.

Small familiar teams are ideal environments for Socializers to function, whereas large teams tend to unsettle them. Small familiar teams provide opportunities for them to discuss their expertise amongst other people who they know well and consider predictable, without the unknown risk of less familiar individuals in larger groups. Since they do not like upsetting other people, they often do not openly say what they think if they believe others have a different point of view. This is counter balanced by one of their great strengths, that being their ability to actively listen.

Socializers do not believe in the integration of work and private life, preferring to keep the two separate. They do not 'live to work', so they are not likely to be workaholics, spending long hours at work that compromise their family or private time.

Analyzers

Analyzers are interested in facts, details, numbers, and especially the minutia. The finer the detail, the better. They like logic, systems, order, regulations, rules, processes, seeking preciseness in everything they do and in the world around them. They do not like distraction, and to that end, their desk is likely to be kept immaculate, not just tidy. Analyzers conduct themselves much like a cog that knows its exact place in the organizational system. Not surprisingly, they prefer everyone else to also act like an organizational cog following the same organizational rules and procedures to the letter. In that way they create a safe, quiet, uninterrupted environment that suits them and in which they can function productively.

Their preferred communication method is to let their analysis and reports speak for them, because they are thoroughly thought out detail by detail, line by line, and constructed in a way to convey what Analyzers want to say. It is both the information and the logical construction used to connect it and to arrive at conclusions that communicates credibility for them.

As information and knowledge forms the basis of their communication, Analyzers can often find it difficult to quickly respond to a challenge if they cannot immediately refer to some information in a report or document. Hence, even small talk can be risky in case it leads to a point needing documented back-up information. Prompt decision making often suffers by the need to have all the information, rather than enough information to decide. The shadow side to Analyzers' reliance upon logic and constructed argument is that they do not trust their own intuition, let alone trust the intuitive views of others. Opinions per se, especially those expressed by others without supporting information, have little credibility to them.

Analyzers function well in teams. They are conscientious and make every effort to ensure that what they present and contribute is correct, but they often lack the persuasiveness to convincingly make firm recommendations. What Analyzers sometimes fail to realize is that, whilst information and reports can play a vital influencing role, there is more to actually persuading others to make decisions or take action. Facts may speak for themselves, but even the most comprehensive, well presented factual report, will not necessarily persuade someone else to act and carry out the recommendations it contains.

Generational connection

Irrespective of which generation you belong to, as an Absolute Leader endeavor to connect and relate to each generation. Understand their needs and the differences between them, because each generation is different. Learn their 'language', and take an interest in them not only at work and in their careers, but also ask about their activities outside work such as the things that they really like to do in the other domains of their lives. You can learn so much from that and it gives you an opportunity to give back to them, helping them to grow and prosper. Once you do that that, you are then in a position to assist members of different generations to better understand and interact with each other.

Do the right thing

Management is not the same as leadership, but it is an essential skill for leaders. Similarly, leadership is a vital element of competent management. Management is doing things right, whereas leadership is doing things to advance in the right direction. Management is mainly concerned with efficiency (saving time and money) whereas leadership focuses upon effectiveness (where to invest time and money).

Using management power, authority and control, is seldom, if ever, enough to achieve optimal outcomes. Leadership requires that you lead, not just manage, which is demonstrated by your ability to influence people to do the right thing by themselves and by others, including their teams, projects and organizations.

Serve others

People in positions of formal leadership often believe that by virtue of the stronger position that they hold and exert over others within an organization's management hierarchy, it is the role of others (especially their direct reports) to serve them. They see the practice of servitude as a one way street, namely that those in lower positions serve those in higher positions, although they may not like the notion that their own role is to serve their boss.

One of the hallmarks of Absolute Leaders is their willingness to serve others, irrespective of the management level they and others may occupy in an organization. Absolute Leaders are able to interact with people at all management levels and from all walks of life. To have others willingly serve you is a lot easier to accomplish if you willingly serve others first. The key word is willingly, but it is also very important that you be a 'first mover' to initiate and take action. When followers seek a genuine leader, they look for what the leader willingly does for them, so they will quickly identify with Absolute Leaders because they willingly serve and support them. When you serve someone over whom you have formal management authority and positional power, you will almost always build credibility and trust with that person.

Create positive experiences

Consider for a moment the following questions. When others interact with you at work, what is the experience that they come away with? Do they come away feeling positive or negative? Do they come away confident or intimidated? Do they come away motivated, or deflated and unenthused? Do they get something of benefit from their interaction with you, regardless of your perception of the interaction with them?

Much of how other people perceive you stems directly from the quality and value of their interactions with you. The more someone else believes that he or she benefits from interacting with you, the more that person is likely to prefer dealing with you. In short, the person will invest time with you because he or she sees that as having value.

When interacting with others, focus upon them and the exchange between you and them. By giving them the courtesy of your undivided attention, most people will happily reciprocate the same courtesy by paying attention to you. Eliminate distractions such as phone interruptions when interacting with others face-to-face, or reading emails while talking on the phone. Throughout the interactions, make others feel that they really do matter and that what they have to say is important to you.

Do not belittle

Nobody likes being belittled nor made to feel in any way inadequate. Even when people recognize their own inadequacies, they do not enjoy being reminded of them, let alone in a belittling manner.

If you believe someone falls short in doing something or fails to deliver on a promise, there is no point in belittling them. It will not resolve the shortcoming. Instead, it is far more likely to aggravate matters so that the other person responds on the basis of fear, which is frequently the motive of those that belittle others.

Belittling is a total loss for all concerned. People who belittle others win no thanks and win no friends (not that they are looking for them). It might make their egos feel good for a brief while, but it can inflict major damage on the other person for a much longer period. Belittling is a sign of personal inadequacy in the perpetrators. Their reputations for personal attack spread on the grapevine and precede them, so that others will be either disinclined to engage with them even when they are coerced to work with them, or they prepare themselves to confront and outmaneuver them.

Be accessible and visible

Having an open door policy indicates you are approachable and that you invite people to interact with you. An open door policy makes you visible and therefore noticed. You are effectively putting a sign up saying that you are open for business. Having your door shut, either physically or virtually, often or always implies something different such as "I am really, really busy, or I am so important that I do not want anybody to disturb me." If you have that busy 'enter at your own risk' sign up everyday with your door closed, people will soon come to realize that you are not approachable, which serves to disconnect you from them.

In the workplace it is important to be seen and to see others. From time to time, walk around and let others know you exist, but use discretion to walk within practical proximity to where others work without disturbing them. See how other people operate, the environments they work in, the people they frequently interact with, so you gain a better understanding that can be beneficial for them and you.

Give praise and recognition

Absolute Leaders recognize the accomplishments of other people. Praise others for their efforts by giving them recognition for the specific actions or initiatives they take, independent of whether or not they produce the intended results. Obviously this does not mean encouraging them to repeat something that does not work. Instead, it is recognition that they have made an effort, and it is also an opportunity to understand what to do next time they are in a similar situation so that they can achieve a desired different outcome.

Be thankful to others. Say "Thank you". However you thank others, make it appropriate in context for them as far as how they will see value and appreciation. Do it as soon as you can after the event or accomplishment that warrants the praise. Go out of your way, if necessary, to show appreciation. Praise people in front of others, or praise them privately. Above all, do it!

Recognize people both for their actions and for their accomplishments, even if what they do is not directly connected to your role. If you know someone who has achieved something exceptional, then acknowledge that person for what he or she has done. People like appreciation and there is a special value when others outside their immediate groups or teams recognize an outstanding contribution that they make.

Giving people recognition makes them feel good about themselves. It reinforces their self-belief, increases their job satisfaction, and can motivate them to higher performance, which is beneficial for all concerned including the person receiving the recognition, the person giving the recognition, as well as the team, business or organization.

One of the most important recognitions people respond to is that coming from their immediate boss. It is critical because of the relationship between the two. The person receiving the recognition gets a message to do 'more of the same' activities that led to the initial praising, and he often responds by doing more of the same without his boss needing to instruct or encourage him further. Contrast that to the fear based motivation of someone told to do something or else suffer negative consequences, notwith-standing that such an approach may sometimes be necessary.

Share your personal victories

Whenever you have a personal victory or a win at work, do this little exer-cise. Stop and reflect upon all the people that assisted you in your victory. Think about all the people that were involved, irrespective of how minor or insignificant the role they played appears. They might have been directly involved, or they may have contributed through a preceding event that helped make the victory possible. Once you have made your list, make a point to contact everyone involved, noting the success achieved and thank-ing them for the role they played.

By doing the exercise you will come to realize that few personal vic-tories ever belong to just one individual, including yourself. Seldom do we achieve something of value without others playing a contributing role. Share what you believe to be your personal victories and accomplishments with others and they will more willingly support you in the future.

Empower others

Most people like to have at least some degree of control over their lives. One of the roles of Absolute Leaders is to empower other people to do so. It is a sign of respect for others and can give them a strong sense of personal satisfaction.

A great motivator

Absolute Leaders empower other people. The value of empowerment is that it enhances the degree of power and control people can exercise over their own lives. People usually like to be in control of their own lives, or in the very least have a sense of personal control. Consider the people that you interact with at work and how you can empower them.

Facilitating a sense of personal power and control is one of the most inspiring and motivating things that a person can do for someone else. Empowering other people to take responsibility for their own personal and professional development reinforces self-belief by the empowered persons. It also reinforces that others have belief in them, giving them a sense that they are OK people.

Before empowering others, discuss it with them, as not everybody wants the same degree of self-empowerment. Some people are threatened by self-empowerment because they do not like greater responsibility, or they might just like things the way they are and do not want what they could perceive as an added burden or responsibility. They might be of the opinion that self-empowerment is really asking them to do more at work but without more financial reward. A way of handling this is to appeal to their values and aspirations, and to demonstrate how the benefits of self-empowerment are connected to their own sense of self-confidence and professional development.

Empowering others does not mean abdicating your own leadership and management duties to others. Although we live in a much more connected and flexible world, people still like to be provided with leadership and direction. Those wanting to follow or seeking guidance need leaders to provide direction. People often do not want to be left entirely to their own devices, because as appealing as it can be to some people, for others it inevitably creates problems. They need direction in order to know what to focus upon, what is expected of them, and how they are evaluated in the workplace. Empowerment allows them to participate in making and influencing those types of decisions.

The role of control

Diametrically opposed to empowerment is excessive control, or more specifically the need by some individuals to try to control everything that others do and how they do it. This is epitomized by executives regarded as micro managing 'control freaks'. For every unit of unnecessary excess control such individuals exert over someone else, they lose at least one commensurate unit of their own productivity value. This is because they spend excessive time controlling and monitoring the activities of others instead of engaging in higher value pursuits. Put simply, they undermine their potential value by engaging in lower value activities. Through excessive control, they can also kill imagination, stifle healthy competition, thwart innovative breakthroughs and reduce the commitment of others.

This is not to suggest that there is not a valid role for proper control. To the contrary, control has a valid place, it has value and is an expectation of leaders and managers. It is the manner and extent to which control is exercised over other people that causes problems. Whilst empowering others involves handing over a degree of control to them for the matters that they are personally responsible, micro managing takes away that degree of self-control and self-determination from others but does not reduce their accountability. People that are micro managed then operate in a frustrating climate of contradiction since they are required to meet role performance expectations but they are unsupported due to micro management practices.

Most people do not want to be controlled, but they do want matters to be under control. They want someone to be in control. Absolute Leaders do not need to know what people working for them do on a minute-by-minute basis. They just need to know that work is performed according to organizational objectives and practices, which also means that people take responsibility for their own actions. By empowering others and properly exercising control, Absolute Leaders free themselves to concentrate on higher value aspirational decisions such as vision, strategic direction and building key relationships. They realize that they cannot do their own job effectively if they are too busy doing everyone else's.

Earn respect

People will be more motivated to do what you ask (and do not ask) if they respect you. Respect comes about by doing the right thing by others, and it is a judgment that others make about your actions. They judge and respect you based upon what you actually do, not what you say. The more they respect you, the easier it is for them to accept your instructions or advice. The less they respect you, the more difficult it becomes to accept your instructions and follow you as their leader. Where there is a lack of respect, people are unlikely to willingly embrace instructions, even though they may be forced to accept and comply with the instructions. When they act upon and comply with instructions, they do so only because any other option would be more painful (such as being dismissed for non-compliance).

Coach others

Coaching direct reports and the teams they lead is an essential skill of Absolute Leaders. Indeed, it is almost impossible to lead others if you do not coach them. By learning and applying executive coaching skills with your direct reports and teams you can help them improve their own performance and the collective results. You can also apply coaching skills with your peers, boss and associates. Coaching can help others take greater responsibility in areas such as self-direction, performance, relationships and managing change. Coaching is an instrumental part of learning and development for individuals, teams and organizations.

Handle criticism

Two critical aspects of effectively handling criticism are to focus upon the issue instead of the person, and not to shoot messengers.

Critique the issue, not the person

No one ever enjoys being criticized. Constructive criticism may be helpful and even welcomed, but that does not make it enjoyable. Even professional criticism is often taken negatively because it can be interpreted as a personal attack. Therefore, when providing criticism to someone, always focus upon the issue, never upon the person. You can show empathy if you like (but avoid sympathy at all cost), by indicating that you know what it is like to be in their shoes, or perhaps by relating a personal story or a story about another individual. Ensure you discuss and deal with the facts and the issue, not the person or the person's personality. Endeavour to obtain absolute clarity of the facts and use them as the sole basis to resolve the matter. Address the behaviors needed for better performance whilst totally avoiding any criticism or judgment of the person.

Some people interpret professional criticism as personal attack. What happens is that they have an emotional 'hot brain' response rather than a rational 'cool brain' response, to a perceived threat. In doing so, they fail to separate facts and events from themselves as individuals.

Often people personalize professional criticism as a means of self-defense. One of the ways they do that is by personally attacking the person making the criticism, thereby avoiding discussion and resolution of the real issue. Situations like that can be frustratingly difficult to handle. A hallmark of Absolute Leadership is dealing with other people, irrespective of the difficulty of particular situations or the antics of others. Integral to that is to assess when an individual who is extremely difficult to deal with, worth the investment of further resources; sometimes there is no other option but to persevere. In other situations, it may be not only preferable but also possible to replace the person.

Don't shoot messengers

The role of messengers is not to give bad news, but to give the news whatever it may be. The news is the message. Whether the message is good or bad news is simply a matter of interpretation for the person receiving the message. Absolute Leaders want the news, especially any bad news, so they welcome messengers, knowing that the information and insights gleaned from them can prove invaluable. A mark of Absolute Leaders lies in their response to effectively deal with messages delivered, rather than shooting the messengers.

Individuals that shoot messengers easily create organizational atmospheres of distrust, because people will not say what they think for fear of reprisal, such as restricting further promotion, demotion, or dismissal (a covert example being to restructure and make the messenger's job redundant in the process). Shooting messengers shows a disregard for people that often results in restricting information flow, limiting innovation, and eliminating open feedback. A major implication is that it can stifle the profitable operation of a business or organization, since because of fear, vital decision making information and knowledge may be withheld.

Act assertively

The manner in which people conduct themselves, be that passively, assertively, or aggressively, affects their ability to function properly.

Assert yourself

Of the three behavior patterns, namely passivity, assertiveness, and aggression, optimal performance and results come from being assertive.

The problem, with predominantly aggressive or predominantly passive behaviors, is that of both types being dysfunctional. Neither gets you anywhere nor achieves anything of lasting value. Aggressive behavior is abusive and alienates people. It wins no friends. Passive behavior also alienates people because others often find it frustrating to deal with excessively passive people (even though passive people might think they are easy to deal with since they are overly nice).

Not speaking up against something that you do not really agree with for fear of conflict is passive behavior, as is usually not saying what you really think. Many passive people do not express their true opinion for fear it is wrong. Even when they know their opinion can be logically substantiated or is intuitively right, they do not speak up for fear that what they say could be rejected or ridiculed.

Perhaps you can remember sitting as a student in class one day having a question to ask, but you dared not ask because you thought your question might be a 'stupid' question. Then another student asked 'your question', the teacher commented that it was a great question and an interesting discussion followed. As you sat in your seat you quietly lamented that you did not ask your question first and get your due credit. That sums up the problem with being too passive. Such behavior denies you opportunities for personal contribution, development and leadership.

At the other extreme, trying to force others to accept your viewpoint, when they disagree with it, is aggressive behavior. Even if your opinion is correct, it does not follow that others will necessarily accept what you say. Losing your cool or showing major signs of frustration simply demonstrates your aggression. Being disagreeable (as opposed to just disagreeing) infers little or no toleration for conflicting opinions, and by inference, little regard, if any at all, for the relationship. It shows an element of 'my way or the highway!'

Assertiveness works best. An example of assertive action is to disagree without being disagreeable. Being able to disagree acknowledges that in some instances, there will be differences of opinion that may not be bridged. It does not imply that different opinions are right or wrong; it simply means that people come to different viewpoints based upon what they know, their paradigms, and the situational context. Disagreeing in a firm, cool and controlled manner demonstrates assertiveness, whereas throwing a tantrum or allowing yourself to be trampled over does not.

Be liked but still do what is necessary

People like to work and deal with people they like. If others personally like you, they are more likely to respond to you cooperatively and positively. Being liked is influenced by personality, but it substantially results from your actions or conduct.

However, liking someone is not the same as wanting to be like that person. They are two different things. We can like someone but feel very uncomfortable at the thought of being like that person. The person might be able to do things that we are not able to do and therefore we appreciate him for those skills and abilities, but we do not desire to do what he does. Others can have different personality traits that appeal to us, but if we had those same traits then we would not be our authentic selves. We would not be who we are. Although people we like usually make us feel good whenever they are around us, we do not need to be like them.

When you do things that others do not like, you will not be liked for taking those actions. For example, if you openly take advantage of people and they realize what you do, that can help you get some things done in the short-term, but it does not make you liked.

As a leader, you frequently have to do things that some people do not like but that simply have to be done. Absolute Leaders deal with such circumstances by doing what is necessary whilst still doing the right thing by people. It is the best and most admirable option.

There is an important distinction between whether people like what you do (especially what you have to do), or like you as an individual person. If, as part of your role you need to make decisions that are unpopular to people who work with you, especially your direct reports, they might still like you if they understand that you are doing that as part of your role. It can take moral courage to do what is unpopular, but if you omit to do what needs doing, you can quickly become ineffective and lose the respect of those same people.

Frequently when coaching I come across individuals that are well liked and very popular with just about everybody, including their boss, their boards, their peers, external stakeholders, their direct reports and their teams. Everybody likes them. What can happen is that those individuals crave the liking of others so much that it inhibits their ability to be firm with people. As being liked is a critical element in their success and part of their motivation, they find it very painful to make hard, unpopular, yet critical decisions that are backed by actions. The paradox they often do not fully appreciate is that they will be liked and respected far more for making the hard decisions and taking unpopular action. Even when they understand the paradox, they can still be emotionally immobilized from making the decisions. At that juncture, they need some assistance to develop strategies to get past the hurdle holding them back.

Make decisions

Absolute Leaders facilitate speedier and easier decision making by having clear aspirations and goals to which they align their actions. It does not make it easy to make decisions all of the time, but clarity of the underlying values guiding aspirations and the purpose of their actions is an important component. Since they know why something needs doing and appreciate its value, they can more easily make the necessary decisions and implement the supporting actions.

What causes difficulty for many people in making decisions is that they have not clarified their aspirations, as already discussed in the chapter on Clarity. Therefore, they procrastinate because they are uncertain about what they should be trying to achieve. Uncertainty causes trepidation and immobilization. The sooner they clarify their aspirations and prioritize their actions, the sooner they make easier and better decisions.

One reason people do not like making decisions is because it involves risks, such as what if things do not turn out as intended, or what if other people suffer undesirable consequences. There are many potential risks and unforeseeable consequences in making decisions but ultimately you need to decide. If you do not, then others will make decisions for you, circumstances and events will force decisions upon you, and you will hand over self-control and a degree of your self-value to others by default. The consequences of that could be somewhat worse than the consequences of taking it upon yourself to make decisions. In other words, by avoiding decisions you will forfeit the opportunity to direct your own life, whereas Absolute Leaders welcome the responsibility and accountability that goes with making decisions and seeing them through.

Power

Power comes from several sources including your specialized skills and knowledge, your networks and contact base, your formal position within your organization, and your political ability. The value of power is that you can use it to get things done.

To have effective use of power requires utilizing all avenues of your power as appropriate. If, for example, you rely purely upon the power of your formal position within your organization, you may limit your ability to exercise power through other avenues such as networking and using your expert knowledge. Alternatively, if you rely solely upon your professional expertise for your power and neglect other sources, you may diminish the value of your positional power.

Use formal authority with respect

To be an Absolute Leader means to be comfortable with power and not be scared to use your power appropriately. In your positions of formal authority your role is to use, but not abuse, your power. Not using your formal power makes you and those that rely upon you less effective and less efficient. Realize that it is an expectation by others for you to exercise your power, since you would not have the power in the first place if you were not meant to use it. The real issue is how you actually use it.

Abusing anything means using it in ways not intended or reasonably expected, resulting in harm or injury to someone else. There are two ways harm can happen through abuse of authority, the most common being to exceed the limits of what is reasonably expected with the authority. The second way is by failing to use formal authority. The proviso in both cases is that it harms others in some way at a personal level. At an organizational level, the harmful consequences are often financial and loss of reputation.

As soon as harm or injury occurs, there is a demonstrable loss of respect for the afflicted party. In turn, that indicates a lack of self-respect by the person inflicting the harm and he ends up harming himself. The person loses both self-respect and the respect of others. People will not voluntarily embrace and follow the direction of someone who shows little or no respect to others, especially a person in a position of formal authority. There can be no leadership without respect.

The proof of this is to consider the 'leadership' of any tyrant. Tyrants have no respect for others, and others have no respect for them (including usually those who benefit from a tyrant's actions). People under tyrants follow orders for two reasons: firstly, the consequences of not following orders would cause them even greater harm; and secondly, they have no other apparently viable option or choice available at the time.

Politics

To survive in almost any organization requires political skill, but to thrive requires political expertise.

Political power and influence

Like it or not, politics is about power, and politics exists in all organizations. It is essential to be politically astute in your dealings with people inside and outside your organization in order to advance yourself, your teams, your projects and your organization. Powerful politicians have power because they are able to influence and exert pressure on the right people in the right places. They maneuver themselves into positions to direct others and to implement policies and agendas by virtue of the political power they can bring to bear on others.

The pragmatism of organizational politics is such that in order to perform well in your role, or to lead your teams, business or organization to achieve goals, you must navigate your way through a myriad of competing workplace interests. Political skill involves astutely dealing with conflicts of interest, be they conflicts between people, resources, processes, structures or between different organizations. A capable politician is able to manage, direct and influence those competing interests to attain the preferred outcomes at individual, team and organizational levels.

One aspect of politics that people generally do not like is that it often predominantly (sometimes totally) serves the interest of the politician. Tread carefully on this path, because if you are recognized as a politician in your organization, others might believe that your main or sole motivation is looking only after your interests, not theirs nor those of the organization. It can easily become problematic for others and for the organization when self-serving individual interests seem to, or actually do, take priority to the detriment of team, business or organizational best interests.

Politics and talent

Highly skilled and talented people often do not reach the top because they do not effectively navigate and manage organizational politics. They find it frustrating and at times incomprehensible that other individuals spend an inordinate amount of time playing politics, rather than 'working' at their jobs. They find it worse that they too should be required to do the same thing, spending so much time playing politics instead of using their other skills and talents in their field of professional expertise. Inevitably their career either stalls within the organization or they leave.

If you work in a highly political environment but do not want to spend inordinate amounts of your time playing politics, consider the alternatives. Wherever you go you will find politics to varying degrees. It is the way of the world.

Politics in action

Political influence is a form of power largely acquired through interacting with others. The astute politician takes advantage of every political opportunity. It can happen in any manner of ways, such as just having an informal chat with someone over a cup of coffee or a quick bite to eat. It happens when people ask if they can have a moment of your time to 'run something past you' because they want your opinion on something. Informal influence can consist of spontaneous meetings in corridors because some individuals coincidently happen to be there at the same time. Other examples of political opportunities include an informal meeting before or after a scheduled meeting; or if you find yourself riding an elevator with a consultant and use that brief opportunity to convey a message or gain some information (only do so if there is no one else in the lift!); or a colleague asks you for a ride home and you get into a conversation about something or someone; or you find yourself in an aircraft with your boss and talk about some matters 'off the record'; or you approach an associate to ask if she could do you a favor by 'having a word' to a third party.

All of the above examples of political influence have one common element, being that they are not the official, documented way of doing business but they are the way business is actually done.

Paradigms for managing conflict

Conflict is viewed by some people as always destructive. It is not. Whether it is destructive or constructive depends largely upon how it is approached. Managed well, conflict can more often than not be very constructive and beneficial to all involved.

Constructive and destructive conflict

Constructive conflict management is a way to understand how others view the world, thereby allowing us to better understand each other. People engage in conflicts because they operate from different perspectives, they have different takes on particular issues, and they have different priorities. When two or more people get together there is always potential for conflict, even when they are like minded and share similar viewpoints, but especially when they have different opinions.

To their own detriment, many people confuse the airing or confrontation of conflict with its purpose and management. They often do not believe that conflict can have a positive purpose or that it can be constructively managed. In some cases conflict is clearly destructive and can lead to negative outcomes such as distrust, lower performance, open or covert hostility, sabotage and an unwillingness to cooperate. Some people deliberately engage in conflict simply because they like arguing and aggravating others, upsetting the proverbial apple cart. Since they like conflict, they create it to suit their personal causes, but in the end it is simply counter-productive and destructive.

Too little conflict can also be counter-productive by inhibiting open dialogue, preventing issues from being 'put on the table' where they can be discussed and addressed. Where conflict is bottled up and withheld inside an individual, it can progressively build-up and turn into major stress affecting the person as well as those with whom the individual interacts. It becomes an unhealthy situation and ultimately the conflict needs to be dealt with and settled.

Absolute Leaders appreciate that conflict can be very healthy because it generates discussions and new ideas. The potential benefits of conflict include that it can help to question underlying assumptions used for decision making and taking action; it can lead to re-evaluating established ways of functioning; put out in the open arena different points of view; put the proverbial 'elephant in the room' on the agenda; and motivate people to higher levels of performance.

Value is in the eyes of the beholder

Understanding the value of conflict is fundamental to its effective management. The value of all things is very subjective, including the value of conflict. What is perceived as value to one person or organization may have no perceived value to another party. When negotiating conflict, it is up to you to ascertain the value the other party places on an issue or conflict. Something may have little value to you but to the other party the same matter could be of major importance. If you apply your own personal slant on the value of a matter before you understand how the other party perceives its value, you could short change yourself when negotiating the conflict.

Value can be defined as the total sum of benefits minus the total sum of the costs (or investment) as expressed in the following equation.

Value = Total benefits - Total costs

The total costs associated with value include the cost of money, time, energy and other resources. The more someone invests in anything, the greater that person's interest and subsequent desire to reap greater benefits both personally and for the organization represented by the person. Therefore, in any conflict management situation, it is vital to ascertain the value of resolving the conflict to the parties concerned, as far as both the desired outcomes and the relationship each party seeks from the situation. The starting point is awareness of what is known between the parties and a realization that some information is not known to either or both parties.

Outcomes and relationships

Absolute Leadership involves confronting people and situations to negotiate and resolve conflicts. Two critical questions to answer in advance of any negotiation or conflict resolution involve outcomes and relationships. Firstly, how important is it to achieve specific outcomes from a negotiation? Secondly, how important is it to develop the relationship with the other party?

The greater the importance of the outcome, then the greater the importance of negotiating assertively. If you are motivated by outcome then you will focus upon the identifiable results you seek. If you are motivated by relationships in your negotiations then your focus will be to build your relationship with the other party. The greater the importance of the relationship, then the greater the commensurate level of cooperation required during the negotiation.

Communicate effectively

It is difficult to convey your message to another person unless you connect with him. Effective communication involves understanding the party you communicate with and conveying your message so that they understand your intended meaning.

The great connector

What do the majority of people like to talk about most? The answer is people like to talk about themselves. It is not surprising since individuals know more about themselves than they know about any other person or topic, they are innately interested in themselves, and they have unique perspectives and opinions about their own lives.

People usually want to talk about themselves because they others to know about them, and in the right situation they ill freely divulge truly remarkable information and stories about themselves to other people. If at first you think this is about the personal vanity of people, well sometimes it is, but usually that is not the overriding case. People just want others to be interested in them. They want to be heard, listened to and understood. They want to compare their life experiences and personal stories with others. They want to see where they fit into the overall scheme of things. They want validation from other people about their own self-worth. They want to know that they are contributing and making a difference. They want a sense of belonging and community. They want appreciation from others.

Absolute Leaders take a genuine interest in other people. It is vital for connecting with and influencing others. If you are not naturally more interested in people than you are in things, that does not mean you cannot take an interest in others. On the contrary, it is an excellent reason for making a special effort to do so! You will find it much easier and more enjoyable to communicate anything with other people if you demonstrate interest in them, since you will subconsciously radiate the message and vibe that you appreciate them. By engaging with others they will more likely want to reciprocate and interact with you. They will also be more interested in and receptive to you.

Being understood is a two way street

When we communicate with others, our aim is to convey our messages and to be understood as intended. We want the other party to understand what we are trying to express. When others communicate with us they seek to do the same; they want us to understand their messages. It is a two way street, the aim being to understand each other.

There is a difference between sending a message and actually being understood. Effective communication happens when the other person receives the message that you want to send and interprets it as you intended. However, what the other person actually believes your message to be might have little similarity to the message that you thought you sent. The other party comes to understand something very different, and therein lies potential for conflict. If you suspect that someone has misinterpreted your message, ask for the opportunity to clarify it so that you are understood. You could need to restate your message, as well as ask the other party to paraphrase back to you what they have understood. Doing so can avoid a lot of conflict caused by unnecessary misunderstanding.

Active listening

It might sound like a contradiction, but one of the most underrated means of communication is to actively listen. People often think that by listening they are not really communicating because they associate communication with something that appears more active, like talking. To them, listening is not an action. They do not appreciate that effective listening is indeed active communication requiring energy and skill to do. It can take more conscious effort and skill to listen well, than it does to talk well.

What frequently passes for listening is that whilst one person is talking to another, the second person supposedly listening is not really listening at all. Instead, the second person is preparing what he wants to say to get his own point across or to criticize what he thinks the other person is saying. Therefore, when the second person responds, he really does not address what the first person just said. Typically, the response from someone not really listening will be something like, "Ms Jones I hear what you say, but…!" With such a response, the person supposedly listening dismisses everything Ms Jones just said. In fact, the person 'listening' has heard but not actually listened, since he had no conscious intention to understand what the other person, in this case Ms Jones, just said.

If you do not actively listen, then you substantially reduce your ability to connect with others. Active listening shows other people that you respect them. It helps you to engage and connect with them on the issues that are of concern to them. By actively listening to people they are likely to reciprocate and listen to you. That helps you communicate far more effectively since it raises the chances that they will interpret and understand your messages as you intended.

Words and verbal tone

In verbal communication, four key elements of conveying your messages in order to be clearly understood, are: (i) the words you use; (ii) the questions you ask; (iii) how you use your voice; and (iv) your body language.

Your words

Consider the language you use and whether your words are: to the point, or longwinded explanations; impersonal words such as 'it', or personal words such as 'you' and 'I'; jargon, or words more easily understood by the other party; 'cool brain' rational words, or 'hot brain' emotional words; focused upon facts and details, or theories and concepts; suggestive of a lack of self-confidence, or indicative of strong self-belief; non-committal and avoidance words or words of commitment and responsibility, and; words appropriate to the situation.

The words people use reveals much about them, such as how interested they are in the other party, whether they like ideas or details, their understanding of context, and the extent to which they keep to the topic of discussion.

Ask questions

Absolute Leaders ask questions to initiate and develop two-way dialogue. It allows them to find out about the other party and vice versa. The more purposeful conversations you have with the other party, the more you can find out sufficient information for advancing to the next stage of negotiation or a relationship.

Some people are not naturally at ease with conversation. If that applies to you, an immediate way to help yourself is to observe people that are good at conversation, then adopt their techniques. Alternatively, if you are dealing with people that are poor conversationalists, by asking them questions, especially the right type of questions, you can help them to engage in dialogue.

Asking the right type of questions helps both parties. Open-ended type questions beginning with 'How' and 'What' are helpful to lead into a conversation, as they allow you to elicit information from the other party. They help build conversation. Tie-down type questions beginning with 'When', 'Where' and 'How many' are useful to clarify details. Alternative-answer type questions beginning with 'Which' allow people to decide by selecting options. The key is to use the type of questions best suited to the purpose.

Your voice

Consider how you use your voice. The critical elements of voice include how fast or slowly you talk, whether you speak loudly or softly, how well you articulate your words, and the depth or pitch of your voice.

To communicate effectively, talk at a pace that can be understood by the people with whom you are speaking. Do not overlook the importance of pausing to emphasize key points you want to make, but do not pause for too long. Pace the speed of what you say, so the other party can keep up to and understand what you are saying. If you talk too fast you will quickly lose people because they cannot keep up with your word rate and they miss a lot of your message content. Talking too quickly can indicate nervousness or a lack of confidence, whereas talking too slowly can indicate a lack of knowledge about your topic, and may give an impression that you are not 'quick on your feet'. Either way, talking either too quickly or too slowly does not convey leadership.

The volume of your voice has an impact upon how well you convey your message. Speak loud enough, so that, whoever you are speaking to can easily hear you (and in some instances so that someone else within earshot cannot hear you!) without your voice being too loud or too soft. Varying your volume makes what you say sound more interesting, and can emphasize key points. If you are speaking publicly, speak loud enough so that someone at the back of the audience can hear you, but do not shout. Open and move your mouth to avoid mumbling and to pronounce your words clearly, making it easier for others to understand what you are saying.

Body language

Body language is critical to effective communication. The gestures, postures and expressions you make must be consistent with what you say if your words are to have credibility.

Consistency with words and tone

If there is inconsistency between your words, voice tone, and your body language, others will detect it either consciously or subconsciously. They will receive your message with a perceived sense of 'something did not feel quite right'. Just realize that in one way or another, the inconsistency will come across.

Whenever there is inconsistency between what you say and your body language, it is always your body language that is believed, not your words. This happens every time without exception. The inconsistency is detected either consciously or subconsciously each time it happens. As an Absolute Leader, your body language should automatically be consistent with your words and voice tone so that your body language gives reassuring credibility to what you say. It is the consistency of your body language with what you say that makes your verbal messages believable, allowing you to more accurately and convincingly convey your messages.

Gestures and posture

Using open, friendly gestures as part of your body language can emphasize key points of your messages and will invite people to reciprocate positive communication and interaction with you. Closed or defensive body gestures put up barriers to communication, making it difficult for people to connect with you or for you to connect with them. If you repeatedly use defensive gestures, such as for example, folding your arms, it can (depending upon context) communicate that you do not want to interact, or that you do not want to reveal something, or that you consider yourself personally superior, or that you are in a position of greater power.

Both open and closed gestures have their place, depending upon the situation and with whom you are communicating. For example, the type of handshakes between people, when they meet, can provide interesting insights. A handshake with the hand (palm) turned upwards usually indicates openness, a hand held sideways indicates equality, while a downward turned hand indicates dominance. A firm, but not overly strong handshake conveys confidence, whereas a weak, feeble handshake conveys insecurity and a lack of self-belief.

During conversation, leaning one's body slightly towards the other person is a positive sign of engagement, but leaning away from the other party indicates a lack of interest. The closer the physical distance between people when they interact, indicates a commensurately stronger relationship. Good body posture such as a straight back and shoulders dropped, conveys confidence, poise, energy, interest, balance and success, whereas poor body posture such as slouching or overly tilting one's head sideways, conveys the opposite.

In trying to ascertain the meaning of gestures and posture, avoid reading too much into any one single gesture. A more accurate approach is to observe overall non-verbal patterns in the other person. This can take some practice and you may need to observe people over time to develop the skill. Another key consideration is awareness of the cultural context when dealing with people from different cultures, since across different cultures the same gestures frequently have different meanings.

Smile

The importance of smiling is often overlooked in communication. One of the first and most significant things that people notice about others is their face and very quickly thereafter, (in microseconds), they notice facial expression including the smile (or lack of it) of the other person. People can tell a whole range of things such as a person's mood just by looking at their face.

Smiling indicates that you are in a good mood, helping you come across as non-threatening and reducing the defenses of other people. It sends a message that you are approachable and it invites dialogue. It sets the context for voice, tone and all other body language. For example, if you are smiling, it is hard to sound upset, since you cannot be upset and genuinely smile at the same time!

Smiling uses far fewer facial muscles than frowning so it requires much less physical effort. An added benefit is that over the years, it is definitely a better proposition to end up with smile lines on our faces rather than frown lines! Smiling also serves as a stress breaker. People are much more relaxed when they smile. By smiling, you will also make the people with whom you communicate feel more relaxed, and they are more likely to reciprocate with a smile. When you smile, be authentic, as a false smile is easily detectable.

When smiling, learn to 'smile with your eyes'. People will at first notice, from your lips, whether you are smiling or not, but it is from your eyes that you really communicate a sincere smile. When you smile with your eyes you make a stronger and genuine connection with others. As a matter of interest, people who have cosmetic surgery to remove smile lines (also known as Crows Feet) from the sides of their eyes reduce their ability to convey a genuine smile and connect with others.

Make eye contact but do not stare

Absolute Leaders make appropriate eye contact but they do not stare. Making eye contact is an essential communication method to show the other person you are interested in them, engaging with them, and it gives the other person a sense of importance. The more eye contact to the point where it is not staring, the more it conveys self-confidence.

Eye contact is believed by many to help gauge the honesty of the other person. One interpretation of people that do not make sufficient eye contact is that they are hiding something, since, otherwise, they would be able to look you straight in the eyes. The less they look directly at you, the less they are regarded to be telling the truth, because, by avoiding eye contact with you, it is harder for you to detect any dishonesty.

Staring at someone is not the same as making eye contact. Staring is an aggressive and intimidating act intended to make the other person feel uncomfortable. It is something that someone does to someone, rather than does with someone, as is the case with making eye contact.

Virtual communication

Communicating in a virtual environment is a critical element of Absolute Leadership, as more teams are totally or partially virtual, or have face-to-face as well as virtual meetings, and organizations become increasingly virtually distributed. There is no avoiding online communication and without it leadership can be problematic and less effective.

Online communication is just another tool or means of communicating, but it is often the first choice for the generations that have grown up with it. Its use complements and reinforces other forms of communication such as physical face-to-face or phone conversations, but should not be seen as a total replacement. Nonetheless, and irrespective of how tech-savvy any particular individual may be, there are clearly benefits in using technology well in order to communicate.

At an organizational level, virtual communication requires the essentials of good communication used in other forms of written correspondence such as letters and reports, which include items such as proper sentence structure and grammar. Many organizations invest significant resources in establishing branding and correspondence protocols for other forms of written communication, only to have those standards neglected when they communicate virtually.

Public speaking

Imagine you are at an industry function. You are chatting with some colleagues in a small group and it is about five minutes before they call everyone to take their seats to listen the speakers' presentations. One of the event organizers comes up to you, says that one of the speakers has at the very last minute become unavailable, and asks if you could fill the vacuum and address the audience.

Now imagine another scenario. You are invited to a morning tea to welcome a new executive into your organization. The executive's immediate boss was expected to conduct the welcoming but is delayed due to a late flight arrival, so you are asked to say a few words to welcome the new executive even though you have not met him.

Absolute Leaders welcome those types of speaking situations and deal with them easily. Indeed, most have a deliberate strategy to speak at industry functions and also welcome the opportunities to speak afforded in the immediate workplace or through networking.

A key to speaking in any public situation is to know your audience and address what is of interest to them in a language they understand. In both of the above scenarios, the workplace morning tea and the industry function, you would most likely know the audience even though you may not know everyone personally. Absolute Leaders are clear about what is important to their industry peers, so finding a topic of interest to speak about for their industry is easy. The current state of play, industry issues, economic challenges, and changes on the horizons, are all examples of topics that could be of interest. For the new individual joining your organization, all that is required is a few words of welcome and acknowledgement, messages that can also have a positive impact upon other employees present. Yet, even in informal events such as the welcome at a morning tea, some senior executives and CEOs fill with trepidation and try to sidestep those situations.

Especially for people with a strong aversion to the public limelight, public speaking can be daunting. It is not their natural comfort zone. Yet one of the recurring strengths of Absolute Leaders is their ability to deal with matters and situations that are uncomfortable or that do not come naturally. Public speaking helps build self-confidence. Although it can be daunting to speak in front of a crowd large or small, the butterflies in the stomach experienced just before beginning a speech is a normal reaction even for the most experienced public speakers. The trick is to get the butterflies in your stomach to fly in formation!

COMPETENCY 5

Align for mutual benefit

"No man is an island."

Adage

Treat everyone like a client

The client paradigm of Absolute Leadership is to treat everyone with whom you deal and interact as a client. They are the lifeline of your organization and of your role at work. There are crucial differences between clients and customers.

Your customers and you

Irrespective of your role and in which industry you operate, or the type and size of your organization, realize that you have customers. All organizations, whether they are government, non government organizations, or private sector firms, exist to provide products or services for customers, be they individual consumers or other organizations.

Everyone with whom you deal is a customer, either directly or indirectly, in some form or another. Amongst others they include: your boss; your peers; your direct reports; your contractors and consultants; your strategic and alliance partners; the financiers of your organization; industry regulators; the end buyers and users of your products or services; your teams; and your networks. Some of your customers are internal within your organization, whereas others are external. All of them, however, have one thing in common, being that they are your customers.

Just having a better product or service available does not guarantee that customers will want it, buy it or use it. The same principle holds true at a personal interaction level. Simply having exceptional expertise, knowledge, or natural talents, is not enough for others to willingly want to transact or interact with you. Unless you control a monopoly, other people can usually buy a similar product or service to yours from somewhere else, or buy alternative items, or deal with someone else. There needs to be value to your customers in deciding to deal or transact with you in particular.

Give your customers a powerful reason to want to deal with you. It is imperative to appeal to your customers with a value proposition that is attractive to them. The way to do that is to demonstrate how through dealing with you they can fulfill their short-term goals or long-term aspirations.

The starting point is to appreciate who your customers actually are, then find out what they seek from dealing with you. You must then meet their needs through the services and products you provide for them. Far more significantly, through your interactions with them you develop value for them. You must look after them and gain their support or their 'custom'. If you do not, somebody else will, at your expense.

Turn customers into clients

By definition, a customer is someone who buys a product or service from you, or your organization. In essence, a customer is someone that 'transacts' with you. In a business or management sense a transaction happens whenever you interact with someone and there is some form of exchange. The exchange will be for something of value, but it does not particularly need to involve money, just value (such as information or time). When someone does something for you that you request, that is a transaction since that person provides a service to you for which ultimately he expects to gain some reward or benefit (there is an exchange of value).

Your repeat customers are people who buy the same types of products or services from you on a regular, recurring basis. In your workplace there may be some people with whom you interact or transact daily, whereas interactions with others are somewhat less frequent. The key is that where there is regular interaction and exchange, you have repeat customers.

To advance the customer relationship a major step forward, aim to convert your most valuable customers into clients. A client is someone who voluntarily buys particular types of products and services, or engages in particular types of transactions, only from the same individual or organization. In many cases your 'customers' may not have any choice but to deal with you, and likewise you may have no other choice but to deal with them.

Customers do not necessarily transact voluntarily whereas clients always do. Clients always have a choice but customers may not. Whether or not you have a choice in selecting your customers, you always have a choice as to which of your customers will become clients on the criteria that they willingly want to interact, transact, or deal with you. Therefore, consider the quality and extent of your current client base, as it is a good indicator of the level of service and support you provide to others.

If you want others to do business with you, most importantly to deal with you voluntarily and willingly, then treat them as customers with the aim to convert them into clients. Try to see whatever it is you do or provide, through their eyes and from their perspective. Find out what has value to them, and identify the benefits they aspire to obtain through dealing with you. Know your clients as if you were one of them.

Invest time at your frontline

To really know and better appreciate what is happening in your business or organization, personally invest time at your business or organizational frontline where it transacts with customers and clients. The reason for doing so is that it is imperative to know what is really going on at a transactional level between your customers and your organization.

First hand information can provide insights that other information may not. Information from management reports and the opinions of others is valuable, but what can happen is that you become too filtered and removed from events and people. It is not unusual for information in reports to be presented with bias, often to reflect the collector of the information in a good light, or perhaps deliberately lead you down the wrong path. For example, the information presented to you may gloss over an opportunity, or it may present a problem that does not exist. The potential downside is that you do not know what is actually happening in your organization where it really counts, namely in the minds and perceptions of your organization's customers and clients.

By investing time at the frontline you will gain a much better understanding of your customers' interactions with your organization. Make it part of your schedule to regularly spend time at your organization's customer service counter or other client interface so you can observe first hand and hear what is going on without being intrusive. Try to visit localities, sites or businesses, where your organization's services or products are provided in order to gain a better understanding of how your organization fits into the scheme of things from your customers' perspectives. With your internal customers, arrange to spend time with them, be it in their work areas or offices, to gain insights to better understand and appreciate what they do. Then take that information away and determine how you could improve the services, products and quality of the transactions you provide when dealing with those customers. This helps build mutual understanding, and most people will respond positively to your efforts to better understand, connect with, and be of service to them.

Relationships with stakeholders

Stakeholders are comprised of anyone who is directly affected by what you do, or anyone that can directly affect what you do. They can be either inside or outside your organization, and include shareholders and investors, government agencies, your boss, your peers and colleagues, your company board, your direct reports, strategic partners, professional associations, external suppliers and consultants, financiers, your project and management teams, internal and external customers, competitors and clients.

Building positive relationships with stakeholders is vital, so get to know them and take a genuine interest in them. Understand what makes them tick, what motivates them, what they are interested in, learn about their background, and understand their values and beliefs. Know what you can do for them, what they can do for you, and what their expectations are in dealing with you and your organization.

Often the best way to understand your stakeholders is to ask them. Asking is an essential element of communication. Get in front of them, ask them for their views and assess their responses. Survey them to find out what actually matters to them, and what they aspire to, so you can understand their perspective and their goals. Only by increasing your understanding of them can you better serve their needs whilst simultaneously satisfying your own aims in the process.

Focus on higher priority stakeholders

It is critical to understand how others are affected by what you do (or do not do), and also by how you do it. Some stakeholders can hinder, frustrate, or block you in the pursuit of your goals and aspirations. These people are especially important because they can affect you in two main ways. Firstly, it can occur through the power and influence they exert in their direct interactions with you, including exerting influence upon other people who in turn might have power and control over what you do. They can bring power to bear on you and influence your success or failure in ways that you might not anticipate. Their second major influence upon you derives from their level of interest in what you do.

of funds between the specific budget items. Another example in this category could be an alliance partner or joint venture partner. In such partnerships each party is affected by the direct actions of the other party, but usually has no power over the other party in its performance of those actions.

People in this stakeholder priority category need to be kept in your information loop, as they can be helpful in preventing potential problems, and occasionally they might provide useful insights as to how you can access other resources.

Understand your organization

Absolute Leaders understand their organizations' aspirations, values and culture, and how these can change over time due to leadership changes and organizational growth cycles.

Organizational aspirations

The aspirations of organizations are typically expressed through vision, mission and value statements. These are usually documented in Strategic Plans (whilst Business Plans detail short-term objectives and strategies), or they can be found on organizational web sites and promotional literature.

Apart from those formal statements and plans, the essence of any organization is also communicated in other ways, amongst the most important being the way people belonging to an organization conduct themselves, the attitude a business or organization adopts to its customers, and the culture of the organization.

Organizational paradigms and values

Organizations, like individuals, have paradigms. Absolute Leaders understand the paradigms of their organizations and they play a key role in devising or influencing them. Consider the paradigms of your organization. How does your organization see the world and itself? Does it use zoom or wide angle lenses to see? Are its paradigms limiting its potential to exploit new opportunities or adapt itself? What is the collective thinking in the organization? Does it think outside the box?

The extent to which organizational values, beliefs and paradigms are embraced and shared by people within a business or organization can dramatically affect organizational performance. To understand your organization's paradigms and values, be familiar with organizational literature such as corporate brochures, web sites and organizational reports. These indicate how the organization seeks to be perceived by the outside world. The reality, however, of how it actually operates internally, might be very different from what it professes publicly. For example, an organization might promote itself as being 'environmentally responsible', conveying that the organization cares about the impact of its activities upon the environment and acts in ways to mitigate its negative effects. The reality of the way it actually operates could be that its actions fall far short of its promoted rhetoric. Conversely, the reality could be that it does indeed act in positive, environmentally responsible ways of which many employees, external stakeholders and the public, may simply be unaware.

Another aspect to consider is how your business or organization interacts with others, especially major stakeholders such as shareholders and customers. What is the view that it holds of them? How does it actually interact with them? Does it trade the interests of one group at the expense of another? The answers to those types of questions are good indicators of the actual rather than merely rhetorical values of your organization.

Organizational culture

An organization's culture is demonstrated through the collective actions of the individuals within it. Sometimes culture can be limiting, whilst at other times it can facilitate significant growth and development.

The influence of founders

For many organizations the leaders with the greatest impact upon culture are the founders. Founders not only establish the initial culture, but also once the culture is shaped and the mould is cast, the initial culture often has an ongoing influence throughout the organization and upon subsequent leaders. That is partly reflected through the phenomenon of 'organizational memory', whereby longer term employees of an organization habitually act in ways far more consistent with the established culture of the organization than do more recent employees. It is also a reason why changing organizational culture can be difficult.

Adding value

How an organization manages and conducts itself reflects its culture. Organizations can develop their culture as a critical competitive edge, acting in value adding ways that competitors cannot match or duplicate, in order to differentiate themselves in the market place. There are many different ways that organizational culture can add value, examples being orientation to customer focus, operational efficiency, learning and education, research and development, quality and innovation.

At the other end of the scale, an organization's culture can also be its Achilles heel. For example, as highlighted in the chapter on Adaptation, an organizational culture that is too rigid and not easily adaptable to change could cause the demise of the organization when the world around is changing quickly. Conversely, an organizational culture that is overly laissez-faire may create problems of quality by failing to attend to some essential details in the provision of its services or products.

Collective actions

Action values, being the values that guide how things are done, also reflect the culture of an organization. The action values and culture of organizations are partly reflected through both unwritten rules and written guidelines. However, rules and procedures (both written and unwritten) can only go so far. They seldom cover all day-to-day activities, so people use organizational culture (or how things are usually done) to guide their actions in the absence of any other guidelines.

Absolute Leaders appreciate that the manner in which things are performed, the actions that organizations take, emanate from the behavior of individuals. This is because the behavior or conduct of an organization is in fact the collective behavior of the people within it. Modifying the behavior of individuals subsequently allows the collective actions and culture of an organization to be changed. This is especially true as regards the leaders of an organization, for they exert the greatest influence by far upon an organization. The more senior the leader, the greater his relative influence upon organizational culture. Therefore, in order to change organizational culture, a critical step is to change the thinking and actions of individuals within the organization, especially of those in the most senior leadership positions. Coaching is one of many ways to bring about such change.

Subcultures

Leaders recognize that different sub-cultures frequently emerge within different parts of an organization. That can often be helpful, as for example by having a fairly unstructured ad hoc type culture for a design or innovation team, whereas the main organizational culture might be competitively oriented. In other instances, different sub-cultures within a business or organization can prove problematic, creating inconsistencies in the execution of its strategies and operations.

Align with your organization

Absolute Leaders align themselves and assist others to align with the organizational culture thereby producing greater consistency of conduct throughout their organization or business.

Being able to live your values and aspirations through your work creates a world of difference, making your workplace role infinitely more satisfying. If your aspirational values and action values are not aligned or reconciled with those of your business or organization, you will find it a struggle to fulfill your true potential. Some of the personal telltale signs of non-alignment include frustration, discontent, and not looking forward to going to work. These sap an individual's energy and inner drive as they slowly undermine motivation and eventually performance suffers. Be aware if any of these telltale signs happen to you, but also look for them in others as they present an opportunity to assist and provide leadership to them.

Facilitate the alignment of others

Absolute Leaders play a vital role in assisting others, especially those in their own teams and their direct reports, to align with their organization's aspirational aims. The more that is the case, the stronger an organization will be. The more that people personally identify with the higher purpose of their teams, organizations and industries, the more they will feel a sense of belonging. With that comes greater commitment and performance.

One way to bring this about is to help others see how their own personal visions relate to the organizational vision. When you help others to do that you can achieve critical 'buy in' from them. The underlying principle is that people need to see themselves as part of the bigger organizational and business picture, so they can connect themselves to it and willingly become an active part of it.

Build alliances through networks

Networks are an integral platform for building alliances. To that end, understanding how they function, and the means to engage in and build value through them, is essential.

Provide value to networks

The purpose of networking is to build personal, professional and organizational contacts and alliances that can provide useful information and support for you, your teams and your organization. People, businesses, and organizations, form alliances for mutual benefit, with networks providing the means for such alliances. An ideal alliance is one where the members contribute equally, providing a similar level of advantage or value to each other.

Organizational and professional networks are characteristically unstructured, their formation and processes can be random, or at least appear to be. They are a source of information where informal influence is widespread, they can change easily and change frequently, and they usually focus more upon people instead of things. Hence, much of the benefit in any network lies in the value of exchange between its members and the relationships they develop. To network effectively, you must have something of value (such as information or contacts) to offer to other network members.

Initiate communication

Effective networking requires high level communication skills, since networks depend greatly upon the exchange of information, ideas and contacts that can only be accomplished through interpersonal communication. In particular, you need to initiate communication, approaching people that will often be complete strangers in order to establish some rapport and common purpose with them. The more you initiate communication, the more contacts you develop, and the better you communicate with your contacts, the more they are likely to communicate with you thereby increasing the value of the network.

Use network information to advantage

By using external networks, you can obtain information that is not normally available or otherwise easily accessible to your organization, business or teams. The information can help an organization know what is going on in the wider business or economic environment, and may be useful to develop objectives, strategies, make decisions, and to grow and improve. In that context, information from networks is a power base both for an organization and particularly for the individuals who tap into the networks that add value to the organization.

In contrast to external networks, information gleaned from internal networks can help bridge gaps between different sections, business units and teams within an organization. Where there is no effective, formal internal mechanism spread across an organization to obtain helpful information, an informal network overcomes the problem by providing access to the people with the relevant knowledge. Absolute Leaders know this and so they maintain strong network bases across their organizations. Within an organization, they are in contact with a variety of people through whom they can access helpful information and insights for their teams and business units, as well as reciprocate the exchange.

Welcome interdependence

Networks build interdependence through interaction and exchange. People come to depend upon each other for information, ideas, contacts and resources. Accordingly, networks function better when members act collaboratively to achieve win/win results even though doing so is at the discretion of individual network members. Through collaboration and the power of synergy, network members can act much like members of a team to accomplish outcomes that otherwise are just not possible individually.

Gain new ideas and new perspectives

Networks provide forums to obtain new ideas, different understandings, new paradigms and new solutions, by being able to look at issues from multiple perspectives. In networks, people come from a wide range of business and professional backgrounds. Each individual brings different viewpoints to issues, because of each person's different knowledge, experience, wisdom and intuition. Networks make that diversity of perspectives accessible for you to consider matters from different perspectives and alternative paradigms. In many cases that may be the essential difference between being stuck in a rut or moving forward.

By networking inside an organization, Absolute Leaders can develop an organization wide perspective from the viewpoints of others involved in different sections of the organization. Through external networks a broader perspective can be developed by understanding the issues and opportunities facing other organizations in other industries, or in the same industry, and extrapolating those lessons to apply in their organization. That type of learning could prove pivotal in virtually any area of an organization.

Six degrees of connection

Absolute Leaders join and develop networks, and sometimes are instrumental in their formation. They appreciate that networks connect people and link them to people in other networks. An underlying value of any network is the quality of the connections between its members, a value that varies between individual network members. For a network to work effectively and create value, people need to connect and work cooperatively because that is an integral element of the network system.

The people you know and the people you do not know, can all have a major influence upon your performance and success. The ones you know through networking can influence you directly. In addition, the people you do not know can potentially influence you (and you influence them) through the six degrees of connection, a notion usually described as the six degrees of separation. The notion is that each of us can connect to anyone else on the planet through no more than five intermediaries. Therefore, by linking into networks you are more likely to connect with anyone you want to contact.

Provide reciprocity and support

Networks thrive on the reciprocity and support of individual members. It is give, then take, in that order. If you desire something, then be prepared to give something else first. Initiate the exchange! If someone provides you with information, she will be looking for you to reciprocate. If you are in a network and you constantly take but do not contribute back in the other direction, members of the network will quickly wake up to you and cast you aside. Accordingly, if you ask someone to help you do something, be prepared to provide help when you are approached to do so later. That type of person-to-person reciprocity is the foundation of successful networks and networking.

Supporting others in your networks is part of reciprocation. For example, you might be able to introduce two people unknown to each other who subsequently help each other. There might be no apparent direct payoff to you in introducing those two contacts to each other, but your willingness to provide support through your introduction might lead to you receiving support in some other way, perhaps through one or both of those two individuals introducing you to someone else that can help you. In that way, the strength and value of your networks progressively grows.

Network value

The value of professional and business networks is based upon the value perceptions of the people in the network relationship. As we have seen earlier, value is always in the eyes of the beholder. How people measure and perceive value affects their willingness whether or not to remain part of a network and to keep building the strength of network relationships. If the experiences of network members are generally positive, and if there is some expected or actual payoff, then people will tend to perceive positive value in the network.

Network value is also directly related to the capability to accomplish what cannot be accomplished through other channels, such as the formal structure or the knowledge limits of an organization. Using external networks to move beyond the formal boundaries of an organization for information, ideas, resources or contacts, provides an invaluable means to do things outside the internal ability, capacity or competency of an organization. It adds another highly valuable dimension to an organization.

Identify career and business opportunities

One advantage of networks at a personal level, is that your contacts can be helpful in identifying opportunities to advance your career, including finding new employment. The vast majority of executive and professional positions are not advertised. Instead, they are filled through contacts, so networking is a vital activity in this regard. Some executives and professionals have such highly valuable networks that their organizations go to extraordinary lengths to retain them and prevent them leaving.

Through networks you might also be able to identify new business opportunities for your teams and your organization. These could, for example, be in relation to new suppliers, new customers, new expertise, new technology, new specialist services, or new joint ventures.

Be thankful

People like to be appreciated and acknowledged. Saying "Thank you" builds a sense of self-worth and it takes little to thank others for anything they do for you. In networks, expressing gratitude is even more important because there is no formal power over someone else in the network obliging them to thank you. Always be sure to thank network members for any help offered or actions they take, instead of just for the results you produce from their assistance.

Absolute Teams

The fundamental rule for any team is to place the interests of the team above the interests of any of the individual team members. This is reflected in the definition of an Absolute Team.

"An Absolute Team comprises individuals who are guided and united to willingly act to achieve collectively shared and valued outcomes."

Collaboration is vital

A team exists when two or more people work collaboratively to achieve mutually shared aspirations and goals. Without that you do not have a team.

A team is different to a group, since a group is not a team unless it deliberately works collaboratively to a common, united purpose. The operative word for teams is 'collaboration', because both the outcomes of the team and the relationships between team members, are vitally important.

Just calling a group of people a 'team' does not make it so, unless the people in it actually function as a team. To function as a team, the members of a group have to act as members of the same team. They must identify with and conduct themselves in the context of their team, rather than as individuals.

Effective team members work collaboratively to achieve the objectives of their team and of the team charter. It follows that the success of a team is dependent upon the ability of the team members to achieve collective team goals and objectives, rather than individual team members achieving separate individualistic goals in isolation of each other. This is illustrated, for example, when an individual struggling to accomplish his contribution to a team may be able to do so only with the help of other team members.

Where some team members achieve their specific team goals but other team members do not, the team cannot be regarded as performing optimally. This is because what really matters and overrides anything and everyone is the achievement of the team's objectives, not simply personal achievement by individual members (as important as it is). That comes about through effective working relationships and mutual support between team members.

Act as a team

Key aspects to acting as a team include leveraging synergy, avoiding individual competition, taking collective responsibility, strengthening the weakest link, building trust and resolving team conflicts.

Leverage the value of synergy

Effective teams collectively achieve more than what individual members could accomplish working independently of each other. Part of the value of a team is the synergy value of its members working collaboratively. Synergy value is demonstrated by the fact that a team of highly talented individuals will often lose to a better team of less talented individuals. By working together for a single, united purpose, a team of less talented individuals can more than compensate for individual skill or talent gaps between them and other teams. They are frequently more successful than a team of more talented individuals that do not function as a team, because high performing teams function 'as one' instead of as many separate individuals. That is not to say that individual performance is not required, but it does highlight that what defines a successful team is its ability to function effectively as a united single unit, rather than act as a group of disparate individuals (irrespective of their individual skills and talents) often at cross purposes with each other.

Avoid competition between individuals within teams

Highly talented individuals can be inclined to focus upon themselves in team situations, because that has worked for them previously and it is their usual modus operandi. What they know is how to perform well as individuals, but, when working in teams they do not contribute as well as they could for the success of teams. The dilemma they face is that in order to achieve as a team member, they need to collaborate. However, collaborating with others often conflicts with their need to promote themselves through demonstrating individual performance in competition against other team members. In other words, they place the interests of themselves as competitive individuals above the collaborative interests of the team.

Competition becomes a major problem and source of conflict for teams when individuals direct their competitive streak against their own team members instead of against the real competition, which is not within the team but external to it. Absolute Leaders guide and unite team members to function optimally for the overriding benefit of the team, rather than pursue the individual agendas of any particular team members.

Take collective responsibility for everyone

In a team everyone has to work cooperatively. Interdependence, not individuality, reigns supreme. Teams become dysfunctional when the individual agendas of team members override those of the team. To promote personal agendas, individual team members might 'posture' in order to gain power in the team and to demonstrate their personal value and contribution. It only undermines the team in the process. To the extent that any individual team member undermines the performance of any other team member, then that individual does not act in the best interests of the team.

Each team member is responsible individually for his or her assigned responsibilities and actions. However, everyone is also responsible to a degree for the performance of everyone else, thereby necessitating cooperative interaction between the team members. That does not translate into performing the activities and tasks assigned to other members (doing someone else's job), but it does require much greater interdependence between team members than in non-team situations.

Strengthen the weakest link

The success of any team depends upon the combined efforts and strength of all its members. Since each team member is a link in the team, the strength of a team is determined by the strength of its weakest link. A weak link weakens the entire team. If you think of a team as a structure with the team headed by the leader, like any structure its weakest link is its most vulnerable point. It is there that cracks will first appear, and from there the team is likely to begin splitting apart if the weakness is left unresolved. It is also the easiest point for anyone wanting to weaken the team to attack it, as for example, by driving a wedge between members.

The weakest link in a team is actually the weakest relationship. The team members directly involved in that relationship must be willing to strengthen the relationship, and to take the necessary action to do so. This is where Absolute Leaders can play a driving role in facilitating team members to build stronger working relationships, and to help maintain and develop functional relationships within the team.

Build trust through open dialogue

Trust is a major issue for teams, since without trust a team cannot function.

Trust involves risk. The more we trust others the more we are inclined to take chances with them, because we do not see them as threatening, and hence there is little or no risk. By contrast, if we do not trust people, then we are not inclined to put ourselves in vulnerable situations with them because there is no personal pay-off. It is simply not worth the risk.

Absolute Leaders 'walk their talk', building trust by doing what they say they will do. This is made easier by trusting other people to do what they say they will do. It means acting with integrity so as not to violate the principles of the team, or the principles of individual members.

Vital to trust is confidentiality as a core team value. Violating confidentiality breaks down team integrity and trust, as the team does not trust the team member or individuals that break confidentiality.

Open and candid communication improves trust between team members. Team members need to be able to say what they really want to express in clear, appropriate terms. For open and candid dialogue to occur, team members must feel that the team environment is a safe place to do so, otherwise the dialogue simply will not happen. Opportunities for open dialogue to build trust can occur in a number of situations, including during the course of team meetings, or discussions between team members in the everyday course of their interactions.

If trust is broken, it needs to be fixed promptly and resolved with both the person whose trust has been broken and the person who broke the trust. The aim is to resolve the issue quickly; otherwise, it will be difficult, if not impossible, for the team to move on, since the lack of trust will affect future interactions between all team members.

Resolve team conflicts

Teams will be more successful if members express what they really think, especially when they have differing opinions from other team members. Differences of opinion can prompt others to reconsider their own opinions and bias. When individual members keep their opinions to themselves, the quality of the team and its effectiveness is weakened. Absolute Leaders make the team environment a safe place within which to take risks, in order to prevent people being ridiculed or attacked for speaking up and expressing their differences. Otherwise people with good ideas or contributions will be disinclined to state their views, and all team members will remain the poorer.

People often do not want to say what they really think in a team for various reasons. It might go against what they consider to be the consensus opinion of the majority of the team or of the team leader. They might think that, by stating a different opinion, they will be seen as not cooperating with the team, or that they will unnecessarily challenge the formal and informal power bases within the team, or that their idea will be ridiculed. All these situations require the team leader to exercise leadership.

Not surprisingly, team members often do not express what they truly think in order to avoid conflicts. Even though such team members may believe they are doing the right thing by the team, the result is that they reduce individual and team effectiveness as well as opportunities for creativity, innovation, and adaptation to changing circumstances. This contradicts one of the very reasons for creating teams, which is to bring together different viewpoints and utilize the synergetic benefits of working collaboratively.

The expectation that conflicts will occur, and the process to effectively manage conflicts, must be highlighted early in the formation of a team. Conflicts are part of the normal course of events in a team environment, but what matters more is how well the team members handle those conflicts plus the learning and progress that results. One way for individuals to do this is to evaluate matters from the points of view of the other members. Instead of defending their own view, focus can be directed to consider other opinions and their factual basis. Another approach is to remain cognizant at all times of the team's aspirations and purpose, as documented in the team charter.

Leadership for Absolute Teams

Commitment, alignment, selecting team players rather than individualists, open feedback, and initiative are all critical elements of team leadership.

Commitment through clarity

Absolute Leaders are instrumental in clarifying the rules with their teams. The sooner the ground rules for the team are established, the sooner the potential for conflict is mitigated. It is when team rules are not clear that conflicts are more likely to occur.

A written Absolute Team Charter can be used to document how a team operates regarding personal conduct, protocols for conflicts, and individual responsibilities. It should include key details about purpose, values, aspirations, meetings, conduct and anything else, that team members consider relevant.

People not committed to the team charter really avoid their team responsibilities. Individual preferences or priorities must at all times rank second to, or come under the umbrella of, those of the team. If a new member joins the team, he must accept and commit to the charter. When significant matters change (for example the original purpose of the team changes), then the team charter can be updated.

Team alignment

As soon as possible, the values of individual team members should be aligned and reconciled with team values. Doing so is an invaluable exercise to reduce potential conflicts that individual members might have between their own self-interests and those of the team. Team members do not need to agree with each other on every detail (small items that do not really matter), but they must be aligned and reconciled to the team's charter in order to avoid working at cross purposes with each other.

Teams and organizations

Team members are expected to work towards the collective attainment of team goals and objectives. Sometimes that might mean the team operates in a way that is outside the established culture or practices of the wider organization of which it is a part, so that the team develops a culture and way of doing things that is different from the broader organizational culture. When coaching different teams across the same organization, I frequently encounter such cultural differences. It is often beneficial since sometimes a team needs to 'detach', to some extent, from its umbrella organization in order to pursue its objectives. This also applies where teams comprise members from different organizations, as is the case with joint venture teams or strategic alliance teams.

Pick team players, not 'individualists'

As a team leader, you will need people in your team with different areas of expertise and experience necessary to cover the scope of the team's charter. The Absolute Leadership rule, without exception, is to always pick the best team members available. In other words, select those that have a proven record of working effectively within a team. Someone who is bright and talented but acts as an individual rather than as a team member, will most likely disrupt the team and impair team performance. Teamwork is the key skill and requirement needed by individuals in any team. For that you need team players, so identify and select the best team players available and leave out the 'individualists'.

Team size

Having too many members in your team may prove managerially problematic. Larger teams are more difficult to handle and make it more difficult to reach consensus between members. This often manifests itself when a core sub-group within the team actually does the majority of the work for the rest of the team. Having too few members reduces the capacity of a team to perform its activities and achieve its charter by placing too greater burden upon the team members.

Identify with your team

Most people more easily identify with small groups and teams than they do with large groups, partly because small groups provide more immediacy and closeness than larger groups. For example, it is easier to get to know all members in a small business unit than it is to know all members of the wider umbrella organization. Identifying with a team in addition to the broader organization, together with the resultant sense of belonging that can more easily develop within a team, is often a significant element of job satisfaction for individuals.

Manage the feedback process

In a team environment, members are somewhat more susceptible to the feedback of other team members. Feedback, provided in a destructive manner, helps no one. It can have devastating impacts not only upon the performance of the individual receiving the feedback, but perhaps, more significantly, upon all members of the team, as an example of affecting team morale. Other members can react adversely to the person providing the negative feedback and might even view the recipient with some disdain. As what needs to be communicated must be appropriately conveyed, a role of the team leader is to address members to the importance of a properly managed feedback process, including the agreed ways to deliver and respond to feedback.

Assess both actions and results

Team success must be defined and measured. Since results are dependent upon actions, it is not only results that have to be measured, but also the actions of the team members. In that way, any performance shortcomings can be identified, discussed and resolved.

Measures of team success need to be on the team meeting agenda and discussed, as one of the usual purposes of team meetings is to track team progress. Information about a team's progress needs to be available to every team member for candid discussion and resolution by the team, to meet the aims and objectives as stated in the team's charter.

Lead through initiative

Absolute Leaders take the initiative to build the leadership and the cohesiveness of their teams. Often that requires leading from the front or leading by example. Leading from the front can be effective when team members stall over an issue. Someone has to make the first move, and frequently it is left up to the leader, in the absence of someone else offering help. For a team leader, it is just part and parcel of the role.

At other times, the closest you can get as a leader to actually doing something yourself to move an issue forward is to motivate others to act, because you may not have the relevant expertise required to perform a particular task. Where it is not your job and you do not have the ability to do it, offering to work with the relevant team member to resolve an issue can help advance matters beyond a stalling point.

Allow others to lead

Within a team, the various team members bring different professional and technical expertise. Allowing the respective team members to lead in their own areas of specialty can do much to improve overall team performance, as it is after all a key factor in appointing them. This requires the team leader to follow the advice of relevant experts in the team, allowing them to make decisions in their respective areas of expertise normally within agreed levels of delegation and authority. Nonetheless, the leader still has overall responsibility for the team and accountability to the team sponsor or financial supporters.

Avoid poor decision making in teams

Emotional attachment to a poor decision, or a leader that does not tolerate opinions contrary to his own, both lead to poor decision making. Either situation should be avoided.

The 'Yes' team

The 'Yes' team occurs where a team has a very autocratic 'leader' who does not tolerate opinions at odds to his own. Consequently, team members fear expressing any opinion different from that of the team leader. What occurs is that the only 'opinions' expressed are really not opinions at all, but instead nothing more than statements consistent with the leader's viewpoint. The leader is told, under the guise of someone else's opinion, only what he wants to hear. Appeasing the leader is the name of the game. When the leader then asks for consensus by other team members on the 'opinion' being considered, all the other team members nod in agreement without initiating further critical discussion.

The reasons that other team members are so compliant are varied, but frequently the risk of ridicule by the team leader, or personal survival (keeping one's job or position on the team), are major issues.

The courage to quit

Having the courage to quit happens when a team or organization knowingly over commits itself to a course of action, but keeps investing more and more in something that it should stop. The strategy is usually high risk, akin to a gambler who keeps sizably increasing his next bet after losing a sequence of preceding bets. In a team, this phenomenon is especially concerning because the pressure to keep committing to something, even if it is a drain on scarce resources, is a collective team decision that becomes emotionally driven. Absolute Leaders handle such situations by stepping back and making an objective assessment, then using however much personal courage is necessary to alter the decision and take a better course of action.

Reward the team, not the individuals

The reward and compensation system for team members is an often overlooked factor affecting team performance. Teams work cooperatively to produce collaborative outcomes and results, but individual team members are often rewarded on individual performance, independent of the team's results. Not surprisingly, this is a common cause of performance conflict when team members know that they will be compensated, irrespective of the outcome the team delivers.

A solution is to link rewards of individual team members both to the collective actions and results of the team. Team members are then rewarded for the success of the team rather than for their individual performance that they would have received irrespective of being a team member.

Trying an 'equitable' compensation method based upon rating the perceived contributions of individual team members can be fraught with danger. Human nature being what it is, when team members are asked to rate their own personal contribution to the team's success, they will frequently overstate their own individual contribution by a substantial margin over what an objective assessment of the facts would indicate. When asked to assess the contributions of other team members, they will likewise tend to understate those contributions relative to their own. They will often give a 'mate' on the team a higher contribution rating than others, but still less than their own personal contribution.

Develop your brand value

You are your own personal brand. Whether or not you realize it, you live and breathe your personal brand every single day. The power and value of your personal brand is what people associate with it, or more specifically what they associate with you. It is whatever your brand symbolizes to them. By knowing the associations people make with your brand, you will know how others perceive what you stand for as reflected through your personal brand.

Absolute Leaders understand that when someone is referred to transact, deal, or do business with them, it is often because of the power of their personal brand. Your brand can attract others to willingly deal with you, or it can influence people to completely bypass you. It is through the way you conduct yourself and interact with others both within and outside your organization, that you are able to influence the perceptions of others in regards to your brand value.

Your brand is the inspiration for people to have the confidence to deal with you. Others must have the confidence to trust you, to interact with you, to know that they can depend upon you, and to know that when you say you will do something, you will indeed do it. In that regard, your personal brand is essentially a relationship with other people, characterized by the quality and nature of the relationship that others have with you. The better those relationships are, the better your brand.

That relationship is based upon either their direct experience with you, or the experience someone else has had with you about which they have been informed. Through that means, the cumulative experiences that others have with you, or more specifically the perceptions they form about you as a result, become your track record. Your track record therefore reflects how others perceive you. Reputation for a good track record commands both a degree of power and authority in what you do, and enhances the perceived value of what you do.

Successful businesses and organizations understand the value of brand value. They take measures to influence perceptions of it, and to protect it, because they recognize that brands can have substantial commercial value. They devise extensive guidelines showing how the brand is to present, and they employ professional consultants to protect and improve its perceived value. Similarly, it is up to you to establish what your personal brand stands for, and to influence how others interpret your brand. Whatever your personal brand means and comes to mean to others, is entirely up to you.

The real development and protection of any brand is through personal conduct when interacting with other people. As an individual, you can apply that principle everyday through every interaction you have with others. Every interaction you have with anybody affects your brand. Therefore, it is prudent to take steps to positively influence the perceptions of your personal brand value, 'trademark' it through your conduct, and manage your brand as your most valuable asset in your career and organizational arenas.

Time is money, use it wisely

Time is the most abundant resource that exists, but it is also the scarcest resource when not used properly.

Prioritize for leadership, not for crises

High productivity results from high value activities. Yet all too often busy people may get things done but the value of what they accomplish can be quite low, much less than what their 'busy being busy' might suggest. You cannot manage time in a literal sense, but the value of what you choose to do at any time reflects your priorities and determines your productive value.

In order to gain the highest value of your time, it is advantageous to prioritize your activities according to the dimensions of value and urgency. Prioritizing for value requires identifying activities according to whether they have a high or low value as regards the goals and aspirations you pursue. The second dimension involves prioritizing according to urgency, so activities have either a high or a low urgency. This creates four priority classifications, being: (i) High Value and Low Urgency; (ii) High Value and High Urgency; (iii) Low Value and High Urgency; and (iv) Low Value and Low Urgency.

Absolute Leaders and crises managers allocate substantially different activity priorities. The stand out difference is that the highest priority for Absolute Leaders, High Value and Low Urgency, is also the lowest priority for crises managers.

Have daily goals, not just a 'To do' list

Focus on selective high value activities rather than an exhaustive action list, as it will help you to avoid the failure trap.

Focus on high value

Absolute Leaders have at least one significant, high value goal on their agenda each day. It is one goal that 'no matter what', they aim to complete that day or make significant progress towards. At the beginning of each day, or the night before, identify one all important goal, then do everything you can so that it can be accomplished.

After you identify your major daily goal and the activities needed to achieve it, compile the rest of your 'To do' list. Many individuals prepare extensive 'To do' lists with too many items that they simply do not have a realistic chance of completing. If you prepare long lists, which you know even as you compile them that the majority of items will not be started let alone completed, cull your list to focus upon the higher value items, but still leave enough items listed to extend and challenge yourself without making matters impossible.

Avoid the 'failure trap'

You can unintentionally set yourself up for recurring and habitual failure by having extensive 'To do' lists that are impossible to accomplish, since you reinforce your own incapacity to accomplish each time you fail to make serious headway in your list. In that way, your subconscious is influenced to believe that you cannot achieve what you set out to do. The more you do that, the more you set yourself up for failure, the more a failure cycle be-comes mentally wired and habitual within you, thereby creating a 'failure trap'. So take care that your 'To do' list requires you to apply yourself, but that you still have a realistic chance of completing the items of higher value in order that you develop a habit of success.

COMPETENCY 6

Progress yourself and others

"A mirror doesn't pick and choose what it wants to reflect."

Surya Das, American author and lama, b 1950

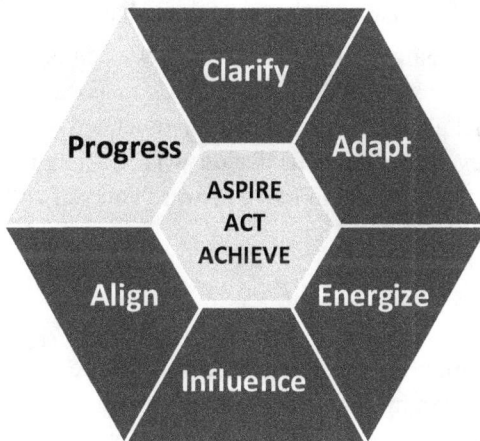

Clarify

Progress

Adapt

ASPIRE
ACT
ACHIEVE

Align

Energize

Influence

Measuring reflects reality

In a similar way that writing transforms an idea into something real, measuring allows you to see the reality of your progress, as well as that of your teams and organization.

Motivation

If something is worth aspiring to and achieving, it is worth measuring your results and progress. Measuring is the means by which you determine the value and validity of what you, your teams, and your organization, actually do and achieve. Measuring is vital to help determine projections, targets and game plans for the future. It lets you know if you are making meaningful progress.

Measuring is one of the reasons why having written goals and targets, preferably in the form of a plan, helps individuals, teams and organizations to be successful. Writing down what you aim to achieve is an important yardstick against which to assess your progress. It can also propel you to persist in accomplishing what you write down, because your written plan is a contract with yourself. The same applies to team and organizational charters, in that the people within teams and organizations must be committed to, bound by, and assessed against their charter or 'contract'.

People are usually more motivated to act when performance is measured, since it provides the necessary feedback to assess if individual, team and organizational actions are producing the intended outcomes. It can also provide necessary information to decide what actions need to be implemented to move forward, and to move forward yourself and the people with whom you interact.

Competition

Measuring or scoring reflects the competitive nature of people and societies. Sport is one example where without scoring competition sport itself would simply not exist. Politics is another example, where the definitive score in democratic elections is at the ballot box, yet in between elections the government and opposition parties monitor (measure) public opinion through polling. Governments can be measured by the amount of legislation they pass, and politicians or political parties measured by how they vote on legislation or how many election promises they keep. Economic performance is another key example where scoring abounds. Share market prices and indices, interest rates, and currency exchange rates, are all examples of economic scores.

Since we live in a competitive world it is helpful to know how we perform compared with others, especially the competition at individual, team, business and organizational levels. Scoring is a means of assessing how we compare to direct competitors, to determine whether we are ahead or falling behind. If we are losing ground to others, it usually requires corrective action, or perhaps trying to change the rules. If we are in a winning position, we could seek to make further gains by taking what we do to the next level, setting new targets and achieving higher performance benchmarks. In that way measuring can be invigorating, rather than detrimentally stressful.

Make scores visible

Scoring and measuring has far more benefit when the scores are visible to those involved in achieving them. Keeping scores visible enhances motivation, because it informs, it creates competition, it gives feedback, and it allows those involved to see the relative position of their individual and collective team and organizational efforts.

The sooner that those involved know the score, the better. There is little point in keeping scores under-wraps, especially from those directly involved in achieving them, since individuals and teams need to know how well they are performing. Relevant stakeholders also like to know performance scores, so, as an Absolute Leader, keep them informed as milestones and results are achieved.

When coaching individuals through performance issues, one of the strategies that can prove helpful is a performance scorecard for the individual. To some, the idea can be confronting, but individuals who aspire to excel realize the importance of measuring their performance and progress. They score their performance using objective measures, track their progress, keep the scores visible to themselves, and they share them with people that can help them and be involved in their further development.

Interpretation

It is one thing to measure or keep score, but it is something else entirely to understand the implications of the actual results. It is therefore pointless to measure for the sake of measuring. Information may be interesting, but it is of no value if it cannot be used.

A critical element of measuring anything of value is to be able to interpret what is measured. What does it mean? Is a response needed? If so, what should be the response? When should the response be implemented? Who should be involved? What would be the implications, either negative or positive, of not responding?

The ability to interpret progress is vital in setting priorities. Priorities can be set based upon any number of different criteria, including the greatest deficits or gaps, greatest impact, urgency of time, organizational culture, and situational change.

Be accountable

To accept your responsibilities means to implicitly accept accountability. The buck stops with you. Even if there is someone else to whom you could shift responsibility, you do not. When someone does not take responsibility for something, then 'the responsibility' does not go away. It does not disappear into thin air although some people would like to believe that happens. The responsibility still exists, but someone has to take charge and claim it. Ultimately someone has to be accountable.

In organizations where leaders do not take accountability, the lack of accountability usually becomes entrenched in the organizational culture. Employees quickly learn to imitate the leaders. This flows through to customers, clients and stakeholders who soon realize that the organizational game is to pass the buck. There are probably few things worse for anyone transacting with an organization to realize that no-one accepts responsibility, making the relationship difficult if not impossible to sustain.

Absolute Leaders welcome accountability for matters for which they are responsible, no questions asked. This does not mean that they take on the responsibilities and duties of others, but it does mean that where someone else who is responsible for something fails to accept the responsibility, then they may well step into fill the vacuum. As with anything, the context and importance of the vacuum needs to be assessed. If someone does not do that, then matters will stay at a stalemate at best. If a person is preventing matters from progressing by not accepting responsibility, then it is imperative that the hold-up be addressed.

Accountability is critical to personal responsibility. By inviting individual, team, and organizational assessments in your areas of responsibility, you will know how well you are performing and progressing. It also provides critical information needed to review and modify actions or game plans at both strategic and tactical levels.

Reward outcomes, actions and ideas

Many people and organizations reward only outcomes or results but not the ideas and actions that lead to them. Since outcomes emanate from ideas and actions, failing to reward ideas and actions neglects their importance.

Outcomes

People who are involved in achieving something, be it an individual, team or organizational undertaking, naturally respond to reward. The basic law of reciprocity is to give in order to receive. If a person keeps giving and contributing, but receives no reward (in whatever form) in return, then that person will be less inclined to keep contributing and eventually stop. People want to be recognized in some form or other for the contributions they make. They want something in exchange, and whatever they receive as exchange is part of the total outcome for them.

By measuring outcomes, we know if we have achieved what we set out to do, and if we are on-track to achieve our aspirations. Results are critically important because without them we cannot survive. As much as some people may want to simply enjoy the journey, it is essential to keep track of achievements so that we know when we arrive at our destination.

Actions

Measuring actions is vital, yet all too often only outcomes are measured. By measuring or monitoring actions, you can assess the success of the decisions you make, since actions flow from decisions. Actions determine the impact you make in the use of your time, with higher value actions producing higher value outcomes. Measuring actions is absolutely necessary, because they determine whether outcomes will be achieved, often being advance indicators of the likely outcomes. For example, sales can be predicted according to ratios. If the ratio of sales is one sale for every one hundred prospecting calls, then sales can be expected to fluctuate according to the number (activity level) of prospecting calls. Five hundred calls should produce five sales and two hundred calls two sales. In other words, more calls produce more sales, less calls produce less sales. It is the level of call activity that directly leads to the outcome of sales made and sales revenue.

Key measures of actions include efficiency and effectiveness. Efficiency measures of actions include cost, such as financial cost, as well as the cost of other resources and people involved. It also includes time cost. Effectiveness determines whether your actions are producing the intended results or outcomes, as, for example, the sales conversion ratios described above. The more effective your actions, the closer they will move you towards achieving your goals.

Actions make outcomes possible. Since actions can be measured, it makes sense to reward actions, not just outcomes. Failing to reward appropriate actions frequently reduces the incentive of people to keep striving towards achieving outcomes. Rewarding actions is, in fact, a means of measuring them, since it places a value upon or evaluates actions. Where a reward system focuses entirely upon outcomes, the potential risk is that some individuals might attempt to achieve outcomes through 'any means possible', leading to conduct that substantially contravenes organizational policy, or in the worst cases is fraudulent.

Ideas, creativity and innovation

Since ideas start from thought, it follows that new thoughts lead to new ideas. As seen earlier in the discussion about paradigms in the chapter on Clarity, new paradigms will lead to new thoughts that, in turn, lead to new ideas and ultimately to new actions.

The same applies to emotions. Since thoughts also influence our emotions, how a person thinks directly affects how a person feels. By learning new ways to think, you can experience new emotions. Once they are experienced, it is much easier to change actions and behavior because of the power that emotion can attach to them. The most powerful things we do are emotionally driven.

The value of new thought can often be appreciated just by having a discussion with someone else. For example, two people discussing a topic who have different perspectives or thoughts about it, often come up with new thoughts and ideas that otherwise would have not occurred without the dialogue. In such situations, the reward can be just a simple "Thank you, you have just given me a great idea!", or it might involve meeting on a regular basis to generate even more new ideas.

Creativity can be measured by the number of new ideas, or taken one step further, by measuring the number of different types of ideas. For creativity to have organizational and commercial value, it must be capable of being implemented. Such creativity is usually in the form of breakthrough ideas that are characteristically unique yet practical.

Innovation occurs when a creative idea is developed into a new or improved product, service or system. Innovation can be measured by the number of innovations, the revenue or savings they generate, and their contribution to the bottom line (or triple bottom lines of social, environmental and financial outcomes). For example, an innovative improvement to providing a service by an organization may reduce the cost of providing the service by streamlining the delivery process. The cost savings are an obvious value of the innovation to the organization, but there can also be an additional, separate value attached to the innovation by the customers who benefit.

Targets, benchmarks and actual

Three vital measures to monitor in virtually any situation, are Targets, Benchmarks, and Actual.

Targets

Targets are the outcomes or results that you aim to achieve. They are the performance bars or levels of performance that you set as the desired outcomes for your strategies and actions. Targets can be set either above, at the same level as, or below, the relevant benchmarks.

A stretch target is usually set higher than an existing benchmark. The aim of any stretch target is to go beyond what has been previously achieved. A characteristic of stretch targets is that they are actually achievable, but are not perceived as being easily achievable when they are established.

If a target is not achieved, find out why. It could be due to the target being unrealistic, or the target not being perceived as important by those involved in its achievement. The aim is to ensure that with any subsequent targets the same issues do not prevent them from being achieved.

Benchmarks

The benchmark for anything is the best achieved outcome to date. When a result is higher than the previous result, a new benchmark is established and the performance bar is raised. From that point onwards, the new outcome becomes the new benchmark measure.

You can benchmark against your own previous performance, as well as against the performance of others, including competitors (either internal or external). Benchmarking can help identify changes you need to address, such as improvements to existing services and products, processes, systems or innovations.

The fact that benchmarks are achieved implies that under similar circumstances, they can be repeated. Under more favorable circumstances they are likely to be exceeded, but that may not necessarily happen. A performance strategy to align people's actions at individual, team, business and organizational levels should assist to surpass existing benchmarks.

A downside of benchmarking is that it only indicates what has been possible in the past, not what is possible in the future. It only indicates best practice up to the moment. To adopt any existing benchmark as the highest level possible is therefore fallacious as a higher level of performance is often attainable, but just not achieved to date. The challenge to break benchmark barriers relevant to what you do is all yours!

Actual

'Actual' is a result or outcome you achieve through the actions you take. Actual performance might be higher or lower than targets and benchmarks, but in all cases actual performance seeks to meet or exceed the relative target. As a measure, actual results usually influence future targets, since targets are often set relative to previous actual results. When actual performance exceeds the last benchmark a new benchmark is established.

Actual is a critical measure because it indicates what is happening in real time, or has just happened, as well as what was achieved in the more distant past. Since actual is the most recent or current measure available, it therefore provides the most reliable, relevant and accurate information for feedback. It provides a strong basis to propose new strategies and tactics. Current actual performance is the one critical measure that does not allow anyone to rest on the laurels of previous results.

Monitor trends, variance and outliers

Trends, variance and outliers are important to monitor. Trends help identify direction, variance indicates similarities, gaps and differences, whilst outliers identify major exceptions.

Trends

Look for the patterns or trends in actual performance information. Once you identify a trend line heading in any general direction, then you can anticipate its eventual destination and make strategic or tactical changes to alter its course if possible. Become aware of small incremental changes, estimate their direction, anticipate the impacts, and prepare yourself to respond accordingly, including what change or adaptation to implement in order to keep yourself ahead.

Focusing upon discrete data and individual events, rather than the overall trend, often leads to ad-hoc reactions (which can at times be necessary). Unfortunately, much economic and financial reporting often does not focus on trends, which are more relevant for long-term survival than are the latest short-term results. A particular short-term result may be exceptionally good, but the long-term trend may nonetheless indicate potential oblivion.

Variance

Variance indicates how far above or below an actual score or measure varies or deviates from a target, a previous actual, or an average. A dilemma in comparing performance between individuals, teams, business units or organizations, is to compare 'apples with apples'. Meaningful comparison requires having a measure that can be applied to all performance and that is relevant across all results. Measuring using a common denominator such as percentages allows direct and valid comparisons of performance to be made between the present and the past, and between actual results and forecasts or targets. However, absolute numbers also need to be taken into account, as higher or lower number bases will often affect the meaning and interpretation of percentage comparisons. For example, higher percentage fluctuations are more likely to result from lower number bases.

Outliers

Outliers are the most extreme variations to the average or trend. They are the exceptions to the rule. They are often dismissed as aberrations because they do not fit the overall pattern or trend. In fact, they distort the trend line so it is often easier and more convenient to remove the outliers and produce a smoother trend line than try to explain the total picture. Never let outliers and the explanations for them escape your attention.

Outliers warrant consideration because they may in fact be part of the normal course of events and part of the path, although not compatible with the overall trend. In some instances outliers can be key indicators of imminent change such as a significant change of direction in the trend line.

Mix it with the best

Absolute Leaders seek to compete against the best possible competition. They appreciate that individuals, teams, businesses and organizations can improve their game by playing against better competition. They also want to be in the best possible teams and organizations.

Seek out the best competition

The law of gravity applies to competition, in that the better and more skilful the competition against which you play or compete, the more likely you will improve and gravitate to that higher level. You will never know how good or competent you are, unless you seek out and play against increasingly better and better competition. It will help you improve your own performance and accelerate your development.

If you always compete against weaker competition, you will learn little or nothing at all, and your skills and competency will not improve. In fact, there is a clear danger that without realizing it, you will lower your game, competency and standards, commensurate to those of your weaker competitors. It is the world of mediocrity.

By seeking and taking the opportunities to compete against those who are more advanced, or are more knowledgeable, or have better re-sources, or are experts, you will be pressured to apply yourself with greater diligence and to be more ingenious in your approach. By competing head-to-head with more advanced competitors, you can learn their practices and in the process improve your own skills, competencies and outcomes.

Join or create better competition

In some instances, the best or most viable options available are to either join or create better competition.

Joining another team can often be done within an organization. At other times, the only alternative is to leave for another organization, and although that does not suit everybody, if the opportunities for growth are not forthcoming for whatever reason in the organizations that people find themselves, then it is a decision worth considering. Many people do in fact leave for a variety of reasons, as for example when they see they are being overlooked for promotion, or they are pushed out of an inner circle.

Rather than join other organizations, other individuals form their own organizations. This can put them in competition with their earlier em-ployer, but it also gives them the opportunity to back themselves and com-pete on the basis of their own know-how and competencies.

Compete against yourself

One of the most challenging and rewarding approaches is to raise your own standards by competing against what you have done before. In sport this is referred to as Personal Best, but the same principle applies in any endeavor of life. Look back and see the best that you have done. What was the best idea you ever had? What was the best thing you ever did? What was the best result you ever achieved? Think or look back to those 'best' moments of your life and consider, not just how to repeat them, but rather how you can go to the next step or the next level.

Invest in a coach

One of the difficulties in improving ourselves is that we are overloaded with our 'day-to-day' activities. When we seek to improve ourselves, it can be difficult to monitor what we are doing and to ensure that our development stays on track. It is not that we lack interest in our personal growth and development, it is just that, left entirely to us, our growth has a lesser chance of actually happening unless someone is helping and holding us to account.

Irrespective of how successful you already are there is always the possibility to improve yourself. This is demonstrated by top sportspeople and top sports teams who all use coaches, even though they already may be amongst the elite of their sport. The more successful they become, the more they use and invest in coaching. The positive correlation between coaching and performance, usually speaks for itself through results and the personal elation of winning.

Top sportspeople realize that to remain at their existing skill and performance level is really to stand still. They know that will inevitably mean someone else will pass them, so they keep improving and developing themselves to lift their personal benchmarks in order to maintain a competitive edge. That is why even top sportspeople, within top teams, have their own personal private trainers and coaches.

Today, in every professional, business and organizational arena, the competition is stronger, the potential rewards are higher, and the greatest sense of personal satisfaction comes from knowing that in fact we do perform to the very best of our ability to accomplish what matters to us. However, we may not know what our individual abilities actually are or be able to fulfill them without some help. That is why working with a coach is an integral part of the success strategies employed by high achievers in any field, and it works for anyone that is committed to achieving something of meaningful value.

Leverage your time value

Absolute Leaders know the cost and value of their time. To value add to your organization, you must generate value higher than your actual cost of employment or Average Hourly Cost. If the value you add is below that cost you need to act very quickly to increase the value of your contribution.

Maximize the value of your time

You can only maximize the value of your time if you understand the sources in creating the greatest value in your role. The connection between time and value is that if you use your time for your highest value activities, then you will create greater value for everyone including yourself, your teams, organization, your customers and stakeholders. You literally undermine your value and do financial injustice to yourself and others if your productivity is anything less than your Average Hourly Cost.

To calculate your time cost, divide your average weekly income by your average number of hours worked per week, then factor in a multiplier for organizational outlays associated with your employment, such as office space, infrastructure and systems. The answer to that calculation is your Average Hourly Cost. If you outsource or delegate your lower value activity items and pay that person or organization a lower amount than your Average Hourly Cost, you have more time available to allocate on higher value activities, thereby increasing your productive value. Against that weigh up any costs associated with potential downsides, as for example, communication with, access to and availability of the service provider, or other issues to which a cost or value can be applied and measured. The net difference is the value of the benefits of outsourcing or delegating.

Spend more time with higher earners

You can maximize the value of what you work on and with whom you work by spending more working time with associates who earn more than you do. The value of your own time will gravitate upwards towards the higher income or value of those higher earners with whom you spend more time. The key is to increase the gap between your productive value and your employment cost, thereby increasing your net value to your organization.

The opposite is also true. If you spend the majority of your working time with associates and contacts that have a lower productive time value, then the value of your time is more likely to slide downwards to their lower income levels, rather than ascend to a higher level.

This value principle also applies to learning. If you want to learn anything especially well, learn from an expert or a specialist, and be prepared to invest significantly in order to appreciate the value of learning, as ultimately you get that for which you pay. Some educational organizations build reputations by producing graduates who earn greater pay upon graduation than graduates with similar qualifications from other universities. Many organizations which have learning as part of their culture are renowned for the caliber and expertise their employees develop compared to the employees of other organizations that do not embrace a learning culture.

Invest in yourself

Investing in oneself is a universal trademark of highly successful people. People appreciate far more what they directly pay for than what they do not. To increase the meaning and value to you of anything, pay for it yourself, or in the very least contribute in some way.

Invest directly in yourself and in your own goals and aspirations. The more you invest, the more you will appreciate your investment and use it to increase your income and satisfaction. Investing in anything or anyone always involves elements of risk, but investing in yourself is the lowest risk. Absolute Leaders invest in themselves because they understand that the return far outweighs the risk. Investing in yourself is the best investment you can ever make, since you directly control what you put into it and the return you obtain. Set yourself a budget for your investment as a percentage of your income and ensure that you spend it all. List the items that you will invest in areas such as learning and education, networking, health and fitness, allocating funds against each item. You are worth it, so back yourself and make the investment.

Give and receive feedback

Feedback is an integral part of the measuring process and can come in many forms. It is essential to receive feedback, and also to provide feedback to others in a constructive way. Informal feedback often happens in the normal course of events. Formal feedback is usually a structured process, and in the case of leadership development the formal feedback process is best handled by an independent third party.

Solicit feedback

What others think or perceive about what you do and how you perform is invaluable and useful information. Constantly solicit feedback from others both directly and indirectly. By doing so, you benefit from knowing their measure of you in your role as a leader, what they like about interacting with you, what they think you are good at, what they think you could do better, what they think you should stop doing, as well as other matters pertinent for you to make progress.

Provide feedback to others

When you provide feedback to others, apply the same rules as if you were asking for feedback about yourself. Consider how to handle potential conflicts that might arise from your comments being construed as destructive rather than constructive by the person receiving your feedback. The issue is not so much what you say, but more importantly how the other party interprets what you say. This is where the skills of an independent coach are helpful for feedback because a coach will mitigate the risk of misinterpretation. Some individuals, unfortunately, do not care if what they say about others creates conflict, as they derive a misguided sense of personal power from their willingness and ability to instigate conflict.

Problems potentially arise when the other party takes a destructive view of the feedback. Feedback that is inappropriately managed is often perceived as personal attack rather than as constructive professional comments. Consequently, that serves to increase the resistance of the person to implement the message in the feedback, the message often being to modify personal behavior.

The next step

"When I let go of what I am, I become what I might be."

Lao-tzu, Chinese philosopher, 604 BC - 531 BC

Choice

Life is ultimately about choices.

One choice available to you is to live a life of unfulfilled potential, experiencing fleeting or occasional satisfaction at best, where you abdicate your personal responsibility and hand over control of your life to others. At its worst, that type of career and life is spent lurching from one crisis to another at the fluctuating whims of others who are seldom if ever interested in your best interests.

There is of course a far better alternative available to you. Irrespective of your role in an organization, your age, industry, and whether you are self-employed or part of a large global corporation, you can choose Absolute Leadership. Making that choice involves experiencing personal meaning and value, not just in an individual sense, but also in the context of your teams, networks and organization, as well as with the communities and societies of which you are a part, plus your family and friends that you care for and love.

In an absolute sense, everyday you can actually do what really matters to you, by living your values and enjoying the benefits of your progress. Sometimes progress may seem elusive, and even involve a step backwards before you take other steps forward. At other times, significant breakthroughs and the elation of accomplishing major milestones and life-long ambitions are yours. The key to it all is not to stand still, but to keep moving forward. The choice is yours.

Your award speech

In the Introduction to this book, your were asked to imagine that in ten years time from now you were being presented with an award for your leadership achievements between now and then. By having read this book you now know much more about the six competencies of Absolute Leadership, so you are in a much better position to consider what you would like to say in your acceptance speech. Imagine that those ten years have passed and the time for your speech is now.

Take the time now to imagine and write your speech. Think about the words you would use. What would you say you have done? Who would you say had helped you, and who would you say you helped? How would you describe the difference you have made in the lives of others, as well as in your chosen profession or industry? What have you learnt along the way? These are just some of the questions to address in your speech.

What is most important of all is for to you to develop your leadership competencies so that you can make that speech. The focus is not about the speech, but about what you do that leads you to be on stage accepting the award. Like everything else, it all begins with just one step. Take it!

Bibliography

Antonakis, J., Gianciolo, A. T., & Sternberg, R. J. (Eds). (2004). *The nature of leadership.* Thousand Oaks, CA: SAGE Publications

Bandura, A. (1997). *Self-efficacy: the exercise of control.* New York: W. H Freeman and Company

Belasco, J. A., & Stayer, R. C. (1993). *Flight of the buffalo. Soaring to excellence, learning to let employees lead.* New York: Warner Books

Bolton, R. (1987). *People skills. How to assert yourself, listen to others, and resolve conflicts.* Australia: Simon & Schuster

Branden, N. (1994). *The six pillars of self esteem.* New York: Bantam

Carlisle, K., & Murphy, S. (1986). *Practical motivation handbook.* New York: John Wiley and Sons

Cascio, W. F., & Aguinis, H. (2005). *Applied psychology in human resource management.* New Jersey: Pearson Education

Cohen, H. (1980). *You can negotiate anything.* North Ryde, NSW: Angus & Robertson

Coulthard, M., Howell, A., & Clarke, G. (1996). *Business Planning: the key to success.* South Yarra, VIC: MacMillan Education

Csikszentmihalyi, M. (1992). *Flow: the classic work on how to achieve happiness.* Rider

de Bono, E. (1993). *Sur/Petition.* London: Harpers Collins

de Bono, E. (1978). *Opportunities: a handbook of business opportunity search.* Penguin Books

Dispenza, J. (2007). *Evolve your brain. The science of changing your mind.* Health Communications

Drucker, P. F. (2008). *The five most important questions you will ever ask about your organization.* San Francisco: Jossey Bass

Dyer, W. W. (1977). *Your erroneous zones.* London: Sphere Books

186

Finney, M. L. (Ed). (2008). *Building high-performance people and organizations.* Westport: Praeger Publishers

Fisher, R., & Ury, W. (1987). *Getting to yes.* London: Arrow Books

Furnham, A. (2005). *The psychology of behavior at work: the individual in the organization.* 2nd edn. New York: Psychology Press

Galway, W. T. (2001). *The inner game of work.* Random House

Gaskell, C. (2001). *Your pocket life coach.* London: Thorsons

Gerber, M. E. (1995). *The E-myth revisited.* New York: Harper Collins

Gibran, K. (1996). *The Prophet.* Wordsworth Classics: Hertfordshire

Gladwell, M. (2005). *Blink. The Power of thinking without thinking.* London: Penguin Books

Goleman, D. (1998). *Working with emotional intelligence.* Bloomsbury Publishing

Harris E. H., & Nelson, M. D., (2008). *Applied organizational communication: theory and practice in a global environment.* 3rd edn. New York: Lawrence Erlbraum Associates

Harvard Business Essentials. (2005). *Time management: increase your personal productivity and effectiveness.* Boston: Harvard Business School Publishing

Hill, N. (1966). *Think and grow rich.* CA: Wiltshire Book Company

Julian, R. (2004). *Managing change/changing managers.* New York: Routledge

Kaplan, R. S., & Norton, D. P. (2006). *Alignment: using the balanced scorecard to create corporate synergies.* Boston: Harvard Business School Press

Keirsey, D. & Bates, M. (1984). *Please understand me: character and personality types.* Genosology Books

Kotter, J. P. (1996). *Leading change.* Harvard Business School Press

Masters, M. F., & Albright, R. R. (2001). *The complete guide to conflict resolution in the workplace.* New York: AMACOM:

Maynard, R. (2005). *Life at the top; triumphs, travails and teachings of Australia's business leaders.* New Holland Publishers

McKay, H. (1997). *Generations: baby boomers, their parents and their children.* Pan Macmillan Australia

Oetzel, J. G., & Ting-Toomey, S. (Eds). (2006). *The SAGE handbook of conflict communication: integrating theory and research.* Thousand Oaks, CA: SAGE Publications

Palmer, I., Dunford, R., & Akin, G. (2006). *Managing organizational change.* Boston: McGraw Hill/Urwin

Peale, N. V. (1953). *The power of positive thinking.* Great Britain: Cedar Books

Peters, T. J. & Waterman, R. H. (1982). *In search of excellence; lessons from America's best run companies.* New York; Sydney: Harper & Row

Pfeffer, J. (1992). *Managing with power: politics and influence in organizations.* Boston: Harvard Business Press

Ries, A., & Trout, J. (1994). *The 22 immutable laws of marketing.* London: Harper Collins Publishers

Rockefeller, K. (2007). *Visualize confidence: how to use guided imagery to overcome self-doubt.* New Harbinger Publications

Selligman, M. (1991). *Learned optimism.* New York: Knopf.

Sheahan, P. (2005).*Generation Y. Thriving and surviving with generation Y at work.* Hardie Grant Books

Short, J. (2005). *An intelligent life: a practical guide to relationships, intimacy and self-esteem.* Random House Australia

Smolin, L. A., & Grosvenor, M. S. (2008). *Nutrition: science and applications.* 2nd edn. John Wiley and Sons

Sorros, G. (2009). *The crash of 2008 and what it means.* Public Affairs: New York

Surya Das, (1997). *Awakening the Buddha within: eight steps to enlightenment.* Bantam Books

Thompson, P. (1998). *Persuading Aristotle.* St. Leonards NSW: Allen and Unwin

Todeva, E. (2006). *Business networks: strategy and structure.* New York: Routledge

Keynote

If you are seeking a keynote speaker for your next conference, or an inspirational talk at your workplace, Absolute Leadership keynote speakers offer ideal topics.

Tailored to address leadership in the context of contemporary economic and business conditions, our speaking presentations are more than just speaking. They are relevant, entertaining, informative, inspiring, thought provoking, and motivating.

We have several presentations based on Absolute Leadership available, or we can create a speaking presentation on a particular leadership issue of your choice.

To find out more about how Absolute Leadership keynote speaking can help you, your organization and your industry, please visit www.absolute-leadership.com or send an email to info@absolute-leadership.com

Coaching

Individual and team coaching is a proven, highly effective method to develop leadership and team competencies, as well as to improve performance outcomes.

Absolute Leadership coaching works because it is about sustained development and improvement, with a focus on real life workplace situations rather than hypothetical models. Results from coaching are usually evident within a very short while.

It is not unusual for individuals and teams to be unaware of what is holding back their progress and success. The nature of coaching allows people to identify and resolve issues for themselves that otherwise might inhibit their full development. If individuals do not develop and perform to the best of their ability then that consequently affects the financial performance of their businesses or organizations. It can also affect the morale of people and the atmosphere in a workplace or organization.

The specialized methods used in Absolute Leadership coaching help people move forward, advancing themselves and those around them, by developing the necessary understanding, personal skills and leadership behaviors, to achieve what matters to them from a personal, team and business perspective. The results are often outstanding.

To find out how Absolute Leadership coaching can help you, your teams and your organization, please visit www.absolute-leadership.com or send an email to info@absolute-leadership.com

Workshops

Client workshops are an excellent forum to introduce key leadership and team development principles to the broader organization. They can be an integral part of developing leadership and team culture within an organization and of addressing specific leadership and team issues in the workplace.

Workshops can be held on-site at client's premises, but are often held at a neutral off-site location. They can be designed for the specific requirements of different management levels. This includes frontline managers, middle managers, project teams, and senior executive teams.

Workshops can be a 'one-off' event covering a specific leadership or team topic, or be a comprehensive series of workshops conducted over several weeks or months. It depends upon client requirements and objectives.

The value of leadership and team workshops is significantly improved with follow-up coaching to reinforce what is learnt at the workshops.

To find more about Absolute Leadership and Absolute Team workshops for your teams and your organization, please visit www.absolute-leadership.com or send an email to info@absolute-leadership.com

About the Author

An instinctive leader and innovator with a natural ability to think 'outside the box', Joseph Tigani has had a lifelong passion for personal development and leadership. His powerful and positive Absolute Leadership program combines motivational and behavioral psychology with hands-on business know-how gained over more than three decades.

Joseph's genuine interest in people led him into leadership and team coaching to enable others to become high achieving leaders of their teams, businesses and industries. Many of his clients, although already successful, engage him to take them to an even higher level of success and satisfaction.

Through courses, workshops, keynote speaking and coaching, Joseph tailors his services to the specific requirements of clients. He has also developed the Absolute Leadership Profile, a rating based profiling instrument used to assess and develop the leadership of individuals.

Wherever you are in the world, Joseph and his team can also assist you. To find out how, visit www.absolute-leadership.com or send an email to info@absolute-leadership.com

www.ingramcontent.com/pod-product-compliance
Lightning Source LLC
Chambersburg PA
CBHW061219220326
41599CB00025B/4690